"By his sound biblical approach to the healing of emotional pain, Fred Littauer opens doors of hope to those traumatized by the haunting memories of past abuse and brings them into the glorious freedom of Christ."

Dr. Walter Boldt, Minister at Large
Christian & Missionary Alliance, Canada

"A book overdue from the male Christian community. I see this godly man exhibiting the Christ-like virtues of courage, humility and compassion as he risks and shares his story so that others may be healed. I witnessed the healing that comes when Fred tells how God revealed his early injury, healed him and helped him forgive the one who intervened with his healthy growth. I pray that thousands of other men will be freed and healed through this book."

Geneva K. Hickman, Ph.D., MFCC
El Cajon, California

"*The Promise of Healing* has so many insightful, biblical principles that teach us not only how to identify the hurt and pain of where we've been, but in very practical ways shows us how to obtain healing and restoration as well. Fred Littauer encourages those of us with trauma in our past that our future isn't dictated on the basis of where we've been but where we're going."

Rev. Robert Pluimer, Pastor
Colonial Bible Church, Tustin, California

"Fred Littauer has the clearest understanding of the dynamics of childhood victimization of any Christian layman writing today. His knowledge is matched by his compassion and willingness to minister the promise of restoration at the heart of the gospel."

Sandra D. Wilson, Ph. D.
Author, *Released From Shame*
Visiting Professor,
Pastoral Counseling and Psychology,
Trinity Evangelical Divinity School

"Fred Littauer has courageously, sensitively and sensibly approached a difficult area of need in the lives of many. With keen insight, he offers practical help for hurting people. His dynamic approach is creating amazing results in a multitude of lives."

W. Blythe Robinson, Ph. D., Psy. D.
Clinical Psychologist,
Founder-Director, Daystar Ministries,
Youngstown, Ohio

The Promise Of Healing

FRED LITTAUER

THOMAS NELSON PUBLISHERS
Nashville

Originally published in 1990 by HERE'S LIFE PUBLISHERS, INC.

Published in Nashville, Tennessee, by Janet Thoma Books, a division of Thomas Nelson, Inc., Publishers, and distributed in Canada by Word Communications, Ltd., Richmond, British Columbia, and in the United Kingdom by Word (UK), Ltd., Milton Keynes, England.

Unless designated otherwise, Scripture quotations are from the *King James Version.*

Scripture quotations designated NASB are from *The New American Standard Bible,* © The Lockman Foundation 1960, 1962, 1963, 1968, 1971, 1972, 1975, 1977.

Scripture quotations designated NIV are from *The Holy Bible: New International Version,* © 1973, 1978, 1984 by the International Bible Society. Published by Zondervan Bible Publishers, Grand Rapids, Michigan.

Scripture quotations designated TLB are from *The Living Bible,* © 1971 by Tyndale House Publishers, Wheaton, Illinois.

Names have been changed for protection and privacy.

ISBN: 0-8407-4919-8

Printed in the United States of America
1 2 3 4 5 6 7 8 9—98 97 96 95 94

I am the Lord your God,

Which brought you forth
Out of the Land of Egypt, that

Ye should not be their bondmen: And

I have broken the bands of your yoke
and made you go upright.

Leviticus 26:13

NOTE

This book suggests a series of adult symptoms which, in the author's view based on research and extensive interaction with audiences, might indicate some form of repressed childhood trauma such as emotional deprivation or physical, emotional or sexual abuse. The author also suggests a course of action which in his experience has proven effective in helping people begin the process of restoration from such trauma. The author is not a professional counselor, and he strongly recommends that the reader who identifies with the symptoms and situations in this book seek the help of a qualified Christian counselor who specializes in the gentle recollection and resolution of childhood traumas. For those readers who do not have access to such a counselor, this book is intended only as a starting point to aid in recognizing the possible need for help as well as the potential for emotional healing from a traumatic past.

Contents

Part IV: Additional Helps

Acknowledgments

To my wife Florence, for standing with me through the many years of struggle before we had knowledge and understanding, and for her contributions to the chapter entitled "Taking Out the Trash," and "Characteristics of Dysfunctional Families," I offer my thanks and constant love.

To Geneva Hickman, Ph.D., for her basic research which became the foundation for "Characteristics of Dysfunctional Families," and to Marilyn Heavilin for her revisions, I extend my sincere appreciation.

To Pam Stephens, for her steadfast and supportive typing of my handwritten manuscript; and

To Dan Benson and Barbara Sherrill for their professional and compassionate editorial assistance in presenting this work in a form precise enough to communicate truth without being disrespectful to the sensibilities of the reader, I extend my heartfelt gratitude.

Prologue

Fred and I did not set out to be counselors or psychologists. But as speakers who have been forced to deal with depressed people and as writers who have tried to give answers to those who can't find any, we have spent thousands of hours ministering one-to-one to those in need.

We never pretend to be what we are not, nor have we ever charged a fee for our listening ears or words of encouragement. Yet we are surrounded daily by hurting people who seem to have no hope. Many are Christian individuals who have prayed, memorized verses and had perfect church attendance. They have cried out for hope and for help. They have no answers for their confused lives, unexplained pains or repeated failures. These cries of desperation have led us to seek answers.

In the last three years Fred has not only worked through his own healing of past pains and rejections but he has also, with compassion and understanding, met with several thousand people and helped them find the root of their hurts. He has not dropped Christian cliches upon them: "Pray about it and it will go away"; "Just forget the past and get on with life"; "If you'd just forgive him, you'd be all right." Instead, he has shown them, step by step, how to reach out to the Lord and receive His healing power—how to become the recipient of His promise of healing.

Because I do the majority of our public speaking, Fred is the one who sits hour after hour with those who come to us in need. For more than five years he has averaged fifteen to twenty hours a week of personal ministry with individuals and has kept careful records of these meetings.

Each day Fred spends at least one and often two hours in written prayer and Bible study, and his close walk with the Lord has been the reason for the miraculous changes in his own life and in the lives of those he has patiently assisted. I can personally attest to the uncanny and humanly unexplainable ability Fred has to reach into the darkness of blocked-out memories and help pull up the pains that have crippled so many, in order that they may be healed. Because of this special gift from the Lord, Fred has been asked to train pastors, counselors and psychologists in Holy Spirit-guided memory retrieval. He has over 300 carefully documented case histories of individuals he has helped find the source of their nagging pains where all other methods have failed.

The survey that Fred reports on in this book has been eye-opening to us and to those who have seen the results. After personally tabulating more than 2,000 responses, Fred describes the shocking consistencies that he found. He now uses a form of this survey with individuals as a counseling tool. In his personal experience and analysis he found it to provide an amazingly accurate diagnosis of adult symptoms of childhood abuse and molestation. Although some in the Christian community are not yet ready to deal with these startling conclusions, we publish them in good faith that one day, in stark reality, people will look back and recognize the validity of our message and realize that perhaps we were a voice of truth crying out in the wilderness.

For those of you who are suffering from pains of the past and are in search of a solution, or for those who are counseling and consoling those in despair, I hope this book will provide insight, instruction and inspiration. The Lord Himself said, "I will restore to you the years that the locust has eaten" (Joel 2:25).

Florence Littauer
Author & Speaker, Lake San Marcos, California

Part I

THE PROMISE OF HOPE

1

"I NEED HELP"

Ever since the publication of our book *Freeing Your Mind From Memories That Bind,* Florence and I have been deluged with letters from people pouring out their problems of depression, despair and denial; of abuse and rejection; of hopelessness and emotional pain. Many have sought counseling, gone to a pastor, pleaded with parents, shared hurts with friends—yet found no relief. Pat answers, platitudes and prayers have left the sufferers discouraged. No wonder they write to us in desperation.

"I'm Ready to Leave the Church"

I need help. I do not know where else to go. I don't feel I can go to my pastor. I went to two friends—or so I thought. Now I'm ready to leave the church. The last few weeks have been a living hell, but this last week has been the worst yet. I'm ready to leave God. I need somebody. Please, can you help me? I don't know what to do and if I go back to my old life, it will kill me. Please, I feel like I'm going to lose my mind or blow my brains out—I won't do that, but I think about it.

I was told to open up the door to Jesus, to open and tell somebody. I did, but now they're not there and I am alone with the pain—and I CANNOT deal with it.

If you can't help me, can you at least tell me how I can put a bandage over it so I won't feel it anymore?

Dana

"There Is a Different Person Inside Me"

Some years back I left the church. I felt I didn't fit in. The members there seemed like a bunch of "happy, praise the Lord" people and no matter how much I prayed, the Lord didn't seem to bless me and answer my prayer.

Once I had the courage to talk to a Christian counselor and was told: "It's too bad you can't accept your husband for who he is," and "If you could just be more submitting to him," and of course to be praying better and more.

Much of my life (I am sixty-one now) I have been sad and depressed and didn't know why. I always thought and felt there was a different person deep inside me, but I didn't understand how to let that person come out. I wasn't depressed to the point that I couldn't function, but I had no joy and didn't know how to have fun. In the past three years I read a lot of books about dysfunctional families that really started pricking my mind about my childhood.

One day I had a flashback. I saw my older brother abusing me sexually. At first I kept denying it. It had to be my imagination. My brother would never have done this. After all, I grew up in a strict religious family in Germany.

As a result of this abuse I ended up marrying a man who had been abused too. He became the abuser and I kept on letting myself be abused. Once I had that flashback, though, I started to stop the abuse. Then he found someone else. Now, after thirty-three years of marriage, we are divorcing.

My father was a very distant, unavailable man. I know he loved me, but I never felt loved. He never showed it. I can't recall a single conversation with him, other than orders of what to do and how to behave.

When I came to the United States, I started searching for the truth. I started to visit different churches and one day in a Baptist church in Illinois I accepted the Lord Jesus as my Savior. But it seemed I couldn't grow. Every night when I hit the pillow I kept crying out to be saved. Again and again I kept going over the steps of salvation to make sure I had done it right. I could believe it in my mind, but emotionally I felt it had not happened. I finally saw a connection. My father had never granted me any favors or wishes, so I could not believe that my heavenly Father would do me any favors or grant any of my wishes.

Elsbeth

"I Felt Like I Was Rejected"

I just got your book, *Freeing Your Mind from Memories That Bind,* and have been finding out why my wife and I cannot live together for more than two or three years. We have been together for twelve years and during that time we have split up three times and gotten divorced once. Two months ago she asked for a divorce again and she has started the process already.

I was so depressed until I started to read your book on feelings and where our past has gone. My dad and mom never gave us kids any affection because they never learned how to give it to themselves. I felt like I was rejected all of my life and my wife was sexually abused as a kid. I had turned my back on the Lord, but since we have split up I have come back to the Lord and feel a lot better. Praise the Lord for your help.

John

"He Has a Real Anger Problem"

Our son Frank and his wife Phyllis are coming to your conference. They have real problems in relating with each other. One big problem is that Frank is in a state of denial. It is always everyone else who is wrong. Another couple, Dan and Audrey, are friends of Frank and Phyllis and are coming if Dan is able to get time off from work. Dan has an anger problem, having come from a physically abusive home. One of his parents is an alcoholic and the other could never see anything good in him. I pray that the Holy Spirit will begin a new work in their lives.

Mary Ann

Hurting letters from hurting people about hurting people. This is just a sample of the letters that come to our office daily, the same kind of stories we inevitably hear as we travel and speak. There are hurting people everywhere, looking desperately for hope, not even aware that there is a chance for a better life, for healing of the pain and strife within, for an abundant life.

Jesus promised: "I have come that you might have life and have it abundantly" (John 10:10).

Abundant life? Perhaps you've read about it in the Bible, but you've never experienced it or anything even close to what you think it might mean.

An abundant, positive, joy-filled life has been promised to all who have called on His name and received Him as Savior. There is healing for the brokenhearted. There is one who came for that very purpose. He came that we might have hope, that we might find help, that we might receive healing.

He came to break down that middle wall of partition that often separates us from ourselves, from one another and from our God. Many of us have built a barrier to protect ourselves from ever being hurt again. We have been bruised by insensitive remarks from our parents, our friends, our spouses, even our children. Never again, we resolve, will we allow them to sting us with their thoughtless barbs.

It's easy to feel, "No one really cares about me. Everyone is so involved with themselves that they don't have time for anyone else." Well-meaning friends say, "I'll pray for you," and you wonder, *Will they really?* They say, "You'll get over it," and you ask yourself, *Will I ever?*

The Promise of Restoration

The promises of God are eternal. They are as much for you as they are for me. You *can* find the perfect peace He has promised. Even if you have never before experienced the love, joy and peace that are the fruit of a Spirit-filled life, this message is here to tell you that you can.

> On the Sabbath, Jesus entered the synagogue and stood up to read. The scroll of the prophet Isaiah was handed to him. He opened the scroll and found the place where it was written:
>
> "The Spirit of the Sovereign Lord is on me, because the Lord has anointed me to preach good news to the poor. He has sent me to bind up the brokenhearted, to proclaim freedom for the captives and release for the prisoners." [Isaiah 61:1]
>
> Then he rolled up the scroll, gave it back to the attendant and sat down . . . and he said to them, "Today this scripture is fulfilled in your hearing" (Luke 4:20, NIV).

Many Christians have heard this good news. They have responded to it. They have believed on His name and received Him, to become children of the living God. Yet despite their sincere commitment and prayers for deliverance, they still feel bound. They feel they are living as prisoners of darkness. Their hearts remain broken, and they see no escape.

Jesus came for a three-fold purpose: salvation, a proclamation of the gospel; liberation, freedom for the captives; restoration, healing for the brokenhearted.

For many of us seeking solutions, life is not abundant. There are problems which seem to have no answers. Suppressed anger, inner torment, daily stress, repeated discouragement, feeling unloved or unwanted, and moments of hopelessness too often seem to fill our days. Does this mean Jesus has failed us? Has He refused to deliver what He offers? Are the promises of the Bible not true?

Intellectually, we know He is faithful and His word is sure. *Emotionally,* we wonder. If the Scriptures can be trusted, why am I not happy? Why is it a struggle to get out of bed in the morning and face the day? Where am I failing? Is it my fault? Have I missed the point somewhere?

I want to know the truth.

2

ANGER DENIED, ANGER REVEALED

After thirty-four years, Florence had all but given up any hope for the perfect marriage. It wasn't bad but it wasn't good. It wasn't what she dreamed marriage would be—happily-ever-after time. I wasn't happy either.

Through all those years we had both worked conscientiously to strengthen our relationship, to build on the love we had for one another. When we both became Christians in the mid-1960s, we gained added tools and resources. We began to understand the concept and meaning of sacrificial and unconditional love. We studied the Scriptures, searching for truths that would help us. We found many, and diligently learned them and applied them to ourselves, to our relationship, to our communication, and to our family. We had all the outward evidence of a family growing together in Christ. And, indeed, we did grow.

But despite all of our best efforts, we never seemed to be able to break through to the bliss we had both anticipated and expected. There was something blocking our progress, but we had no idea what it could be. We became resigned to living out life as we knew it. The joy, the sparkle, the flame had all but died.

I was frustrated, often feeling Florence didn't really love me. I had cried out to God, *Why do I have to be married to a woman who doesn't seem to love me? To a woman who refuses to try to meet my needs, to even talk with me about my deeper feelings?* We were both struggling, yet always trying to practice biblical principles to make our relationship work. We never gave up trying, but in truth, neither of us really expected the other would ever improve. We each simply tried to do our part, hoping by faith and obedience for changes.

The Cruise of a Lifetime

By July of 1987, I began to feel there had been some real progress. I felt better about myself and because I was diligently practicing the clear principles of Scripture I had studied, there seemed to be hope.

At the end of the month, Florence and I, with our daughter Marita and our friend Lana Bateman, were leading a group of sixty Christians aboard the Cunard Princess on a seven-day Alaskan cruise. As part of the program, we were going to be conducting daily workshops aboard the ship. We had all eagerly looked forward to this fun-filled ministry/vacation.

Everyone flew into Anchorage for our assembly and three-hour train ride to Whittier, the point of embarkation on the coast. The train ride was fun. We enjoyed meeting one another, getting acquainted and seeing first-time views of some of the Alaskan shoreline. As the train finally rolled to the end of the line, we were stunned at the sight of Whittier. This was no exotic port one sees in the travel brochures. This was no "Love Boat" departure. There were no waving crowds, bands or streamers to make the occasion festive. Whittier looked like a deserted military post. In fact, we later discovered this is what it was—a relic from the war of the '40s, with stark, grey square concrete blocks for the few buildings. Alongside the dull, dilapidated railway warehouse was our bright, white sparkling home for seven days and six nights, looking totally out of place. Modern passenger baggage handling hadn't yet come to the wilderness wharf. It was several hours before the last suitcase and city sailor were securely aboard, and the ship slid out to the seas on our leisurely cruise southward.

Once our cruise clothes were unpacked in our cabin and our suitcases stowed, we gathered to review our individual workshop responsibilities and assignments. I had planned the cruise from the start and we had agreed that basically I would be in charge. Even our own ship could only steer successfully with one captain.

In our meeting, Florence asked me if there was something I particularly wanted to speak on. I offered that I already had planned to share a segment on "How to Meet Your Mate's Emotional Needs," a topic I had a lot of feeling for and had already done a few times with positive results.

Florence replied, "You can't teach something you haven't learned to do yourself."

What? I was dumbfounded! I couldn't believe what I had heard. I thought I had been doing so well. I thought we had made good progress. I frankly thought I had made more progress than she had. I sat there saying nothing, trying to act as if nothing had happened. But inside I was in turmoil.

All right, I decided, *that's fine. I don't need to speak. I'll just take care of my responsibilities, and make sure the lounge on the deck is rearranged each morning for the meetings and that everything is in order.*

I felt I did a very nice job of hiding my feelings. I just stuffed the hurt away, and displayed the peace of God which passes understanding. I would not let self-centered ego get in the way of what we had planned to be a fun time.

But, wait a minute. Wasn't it agreed that since I had planned everything, I would be captain this week? That didn't seem to add up. I certainly wasn't in charge here. Though I began to feel more and more troubled, I decided to not let my hurt feelings interfere with what we felt the Lord had called us to do. My "light would shine in the midst of this crooked and perverse generation."

As the cruise wore on, I realized more and more that I was not happy. I didn't have peace. I continued to hide, quite successfully I thought, how miserable I was. I secluded myself in prayer. I sought solace in the Word. I did everything that my twenty-three years' experience as a Christian taught me. But any respite was only temporary.

The ocean outside was calm and blue. The sky sparkled both day and night. The Alaskan coastline and glaciers were spectacular. The ports of call, Skagway, Juneau and Ketchikan, were fun and the local history was fascinating. Aboard ship the food and dining were everything we had anticipated. The workshops were well attended and went superbly. I sat stoically in the back, participating cheerfully but only when called upon.

But I was becoming more miserable all the time, working harder and harder to hide it, having no idea that anyone noticed my growing gloom. As host of our group I thought it my responsibility to make sure everyone was enjoying themselves, to make them feel wanted and glad they came. But how could I do that when I didn't feel wanted myself? I was trapped on board for seven days. I vowed, *Never again. I will never again go on a cruise where I can't get off.* I spent more and more time alone.

As I became more withdrawn, Florence spent less time with me. This only made me feel more misunderstood and unwanted. She never once asked me, "Is there something wrong? Is there something bothering you?" In the past, I would have answered, "No, nothing. Why?"

Had she asked me this time, I was ready. I was going to tell her. How could she have said such a thing? *"You can't teach something you haven't learned yourself."* Didn't she know what that did to me? It wasn't even a discussion. She just made a flat statement. Where did she get the right to accuse? This mess was her fault. If she hadn't made such a cutting pronouncement, if she had even discussed it with me . . . but no. I just felt shut out—from the conference, from the peoples' lives, and ultimately from all the fun.

The Meeting That Changed My Life

Friday afternoon the ship was cruising south through the straits. We would be docking in Vancouver the next morning, and the cruise would be over. Florence found me and said she needed to talk with me. Along came Marita and Lana. We went to our cramped little cabin. This was going to be some meeting.

Florence began by telling me there was something in me that she couldn't live with any longer. Something in me? Wasn't she the one who had made the remark? Wasn't she the one who was not meeting my needs?

Again, keeping my own feelings completely bottled up, I commended myself for being so noble. Always the gentleman, I let her go on.

My wife proceeded to tell me that I have a lot of anger in me, and that I need to do something about it. Me, angry? I have no anger. I have never, ever exploded at her. I have never hit her. I don't think I ever yelled at her. How could she say I have anger in me?

Instantly, my mental and emotional defenses went to work and I convinced myself she was totally wrong. She had never understood me, never given me the love I wanted and felt I was entitled to. I had never received it as a child and my marriage was no different. Outwardly, I just sat there and took it, saying little. I was beginning to get upset. I, the innocent party, was being attacked by the one who had wronged me.

Florence continued, saying I needed to find someone who could help me see my anger and show me what to do about it. What anger? I still insisted to myself I had no anger. If anything was true, it was just the reverse. Hadn't the Lord given me His perfect peace as He had promised?

> Peace I leave with you, My peace I give unto you: not as the world giveth, give I unto you. Let not your heart be troubled, neither let it be afraid (John 14:27).

That was one of my favorite verses. I had memorized it. I had applied and realized it in my life. I didn't have anger. I had the peace of God. What was she talking about? She didn't know me at all. She didn't know the *real* me. She hadn't even noticed the great work the Lord had been doing in my life. She hadn't even seen that I was a man of God, that I handled stress and problems well, that I never was afraid, that I rarely worried.

Worse yet, the three of them told me I was in denial. They said I was not willing to look at myself and see who I really was. Wrong again! All my life I have diligently worked on my character and personality. Any time I sensed a weakness, I would focus on it, trying to become a better person. Anytime I upset someone or someone upset me, I would analyze it and search the Scriptures for an answer. Then I would apply it to myself. I was growing in my Christian life. I was improving. So what was happening here? This was unbelievable!

The more I thought about this scene in our cabin and how unfair and ridiculous it was—three against one—I began to boil inside. I could feel it coming up. I was getting mad. I was angry!

Angry?

Yes, I was angry. Was it possible? Could they be right? Was it true that there was anger in me? As these thoughts raced through my mind, I tried to grasp what was being said.

Suddenly, a calm came over me. Instantly I knew what it was. It was the Holy Spirit quieting my shattered emotions. I became willing to listen. I became willing to hear what they were telling me. I heard myself say, "All right, if you see anger in me, I am willing to go to someone who can help me." I would never have believed I'd say those words. I never thought I needed counseling. I had thought it was Florence who needed the help, but here I was agreeing to go.

I thought that should have been enough. I had gotten the message. I had been quieted by the Spirit, and I had agreed to seek help. Enough. Why drag it on? But they wanted to be sure I got the message. They continued to hammer more nails into the box they had built for me. I just sat and listened, feeling alone, unloved and misunderstood. Before the three of them left me in the little shipboard cabin, Lana said, "And Fred, suicide is not the answer."

I quickly agreed with feigned bravado, "Oh, no, I would never think of anything like that."

Surviving the Aftermath

The next hour may well have been the worst of my conscious memory. I sat in the cabin for a while after they left, digesting what they had dished out to me. It wasn't very pleasant. Those old feelings of being unloved, misunderstood and overlooked began to flair up.

I went up on deck to get some air. Maybe a change of scenery would get my eyes off my hurts and make me feel better.

I strolled to the afterdeck, stood at the rail and looked down to the sea of foam that was being churned up by the ship's full-thrust propellers. I wondered how far down it was. Could I survive a jump? I looked to the shores on both sides as the ship plowed through the inside strait. The shoreline was thick with forests right up to the water's edge. I'm a good swimmer and a good diver. I estimated the distance to the shorelines. It must have been over a mile on each side. Would I make it? What was the temperature of the water? Would I freeze? I didn't really like the idea of drowning. What if I did make it to the shore? My clothes would be wet and there wasn't a soul to be seen for miles, no one to help me. I would be alone, no better off than right now.

I looked around. There was no one on the deck. If I jumped and no one saw me, and if I couldn't make it, there would be no chance for help. I would just see the ship rapidly disappear in the distance. Florence would wonder where I was. She would look for me, but she wouldn't find me. I would be gone. No one would know where, when or how. I only wanted to jump if I was sure I could make it to shore. I wasn't sure. If I didn't make it, the only alternative was . . .

What was I thinking of? I heard Lana's words again, "And Fred, suicide is not the answer." The Lord must have given her those words at that moment. Again, I heard my reply, "Oh no, I would never think of anything like that."

Here I was, thinking of that very thing! Thinking of jumping a hundred feet or more from a big ocean liner moving at full speed into churning, frigid water. That would be suicide! There would be no chance of making it to shore. Even under the best of conditions, I doubted I had the strength to swim that distance.

I turned away from the ship's rail, lest a wave of emotion overtake me and . . . I couldn't think of it, it was too horrible.

That was too close. For the first time in my life I had actually considered escape from all my pains and frustrations. The closest I had come to "escape" before was thinking of running away from home as a little boy. I didn't do it then, either. How would I survive? What would my mother and father think? How would they feel? I couldn't do that to them then, and I couldn't do it to Florence now. I walked back inside, back into safety. I wandered the decks aimlessly. The rest has all become a blur.

A Turning Point

Less than three weeks later: August 12, 1987. This day was the turning point of my entire life. Fifty-eight years had slipped away, with little accomplished, little to show, much frustration and much disappointment. I had life eternal, but it had not been abundant, and until this day there seemed little chance that it ever would be.

Florence and I were in Charlotte, North Carolina at the television studio of what was the old PTL Club. Gary McSpadden was the host. We were sitting in the anteroom, waiting for our turn to go on the set. The television set in the corner was on. I got up, walked over and turned the dial to see what else might be on. Suddenly a familiar face flashed on the screen. It was our good friend Becky Tirabassi. She was on the Joy show with Jim McClelland, coming from the Trinity Broadcasting Network in Costa Mesa, California. I called to Florence, "Look, honey, Becky's on the Joy show."

We have known Becky for several years. The Lord has done some amazing things in her life through prayer, which she describes in her new book, *Let Prayer Change Your Life.* Becky spends an hour a day writing out her prayers, word for word, and I always thought it was great that the Lord led her to do that. I preferred to spend more time in Bible study; I enjoyed digging out deeper truths from the Word. Prayer? I prayed, but I could hardly say it was the foundation of my Christian life.

That morning I listened as Becky once again shared her daily discipline of written prayer. Suddenly, a message came to me, clear as could be. I was to do the same thing. I was to write my prayers. There was no question of the message or where it came from!

The next afternoon we flew to Boston, the city of Florence's roots, to spend a couple of days before going on to Maine for a week's vacation. While in Boston, I found a stationery store and bought an 8-1/2" x 11" spiral notebook. This was to be my prayer notebook.

Tuesday morning, August 18, 1987, after breakfast, Florence and I were sitting in our little cabin, overlooking Little Sebago Lake. The sun was shining on this warm, beautiful day. After spending some time studying in James, I took up my prayer book for the very first time and started to write. I wrote and I wrote. My prayer came so fast I could hardly keep up. That first day I prayed for about an hour and a half—four full pages! I had never prayed before for more than five minutes. For a full hour and a half my mind was fixed on God. I started by confessing, getting out the garbage, and ended in joyful praise. Here is part of the exact petition I brought before the Lord that day:

> O Lord, my God, I thank you today especially for the Bible, Your perfect Word that shows where I have strayed in my efforts and desire to please You, to be holy, to live a righteous and exemplary life. Lord, I pray that you will show me all the selfish and self-centered attitudes that creep into my thinking, those things that cause even minor disruptions in the harmony You have both prescribed and provided for me with Florence.
>
> Lord, this morning you have shown me that had I remembered to pray, "Lord, help me" (a key prayer over the years for me from Matthew 15:25), on that Alaskan cruise three weeks ago, what a different result there could have been. I was bathed in anger, frustration and hurt feelings. My focus was totally on myself, not on my Lord Jesus, not on doing everything I could to please my wife and to assist her in the ministry to which you have called her. Despite *my efforts* to be cleansed and healed by prayer and study, I failed—so deeply in the grip of self was I.
>
> Forgive me, O God. I was wrong. I was self-centered. So much so that it never occurred to me to pray, "Lord, help me." I know You would have answered that prayer. Everyone could see how miserable I was making myself and everyone else. Only I couldn't see it. I thought I was wearing a happy face but only fooled myself.
>
> My daughter avoided me and finally told me I was pathetic. That one-two punch from my wife and then my daughter was too much for me. I am not as strong spiritually as I thought. I had no resources to draw upon. There seemed to be no reason to live, and yet I knew there was.
>
> Thank You, O God, for allowing me to experience that horrible week so that I could see my own spiritual depravity. I was helpless to bring myself out of it, until You, the

Holy Spirit, quieted my soul and I could see that I needed to listen.

The love, the tenderness, the feeling that I have craved from my wife has grown stronger each day. We enjoy each other's company and it is like a honeymoon. Thank You, O God, for lifting me out of the pit of selfishness. Thank you, dear Lord, for the confirmation of what I have been teaching, that selfishness is the cause of all quarrel and conflict as I found today in James 4:1. How that encouraged my heart to see in Scripture that which I knew to be true.

Dear Jesus, let me not forget that truth and to apply it to myself. Let me be the selfless and spiritual husband for my wife that she desires, and that I know You desire also.

Now each morning, six and a half years later, I still spend an hour to an hour and a half with the Lord, in my private prayer closet. Generally I study first in the Scriptures, and then spend intimate time with the Lord in written prayer. There is no question in my mind that it is the foundation of everything that has happened in my life since that turning point. As long as I remain on this earth, I am committed to maintain this daily discipline. The blessings and rewards that His fountain has poured on me are far beyond what I could ever hope.

With this new discipline of prayer to shore me up, I was better prepared for the next wave of discoveries.

3

DISCOVERING THE SOURCE OF THE HURT

In December of that year, as I had agreed with Florence, I spent two and a half weeks in intensive counseling, four hours a day. Feelings that had been suppressed for years and years were allowed to be expressed. I learned that feelings which had developed during my childhood significantly affected my adult attitudes and behavior. I also learned that feelings and emotions are God-given and they are not wrong; they can be appropriately expressed.

I could see that as a child, I never felt loved or valued. It was clear that I brought this deep, empty chasm into my marriage. I expected the one person who was to be the focus of the rest of my life to cheerfully and continually spend her days filling what proved to be a bottomless pit.

Needless to say, Florence soon tired of that game. When she pulled back, I naturally felt unloved. These feelings triggered deep hurts and resentments from my childhood that I didn't even know existed. Hurts became frustrations, and frustrations became anger. Yes, the anger was there, and now knowing where it came from gave me the ability to deal with it.

I knew my parents loved me. They always worked hard to provide for me, my three brothers and my sister. The problem was that although I knew intellectually that I was loved, I didn't feel emotionally that I was loved. I was a victim of *rejection.* I had heard the term, but I never dreamed it applied to me. I have since learned that most everyone of us to varying degrees are victims of rejection. It affects people differently and several members of the same family will react and respond differently because of varying ages, personalities and experiences.

As my counselor continued to probe my feelings and emotions, I acknowledged many which were labeled "sexual compulsions." They had begun in my early teen years and continued on into my adult life. I can't remember when they first started—possibly as early as age ten or eleven.

As I studied my own childhood, I was surprised to learn that my memories are not as clear as I thought. The memories of my school years are very clear. I could take you today, back to Henry Barnard School in New Rochelle, New York, and as we walk through the school I could point out every classroom from afternoon kindergarten through the seventh grade. I could name and describe every teacher, and in most, if not all of the rooms show you my desk. I can even see myself standing in the big cloak room in the first grade where Mrs. Leutner sent me a couple of times when I was "out of order."

School was basically a happy place for me. I liked my teachers and I did my work well. In the earlier years peer relationships with boys and girls were relatively normal. Gradually I began to feel more and more isolated and overlooked. I now recognize that this little boy was so craving for attention and recognition to make up for the nurturing he was not getting at home that he was subtly and unknowingly pushing his friends away. Wasn't this the same pattern I had now repeated in my marriage? I married for the specific purpose of cementing a relationship with someone who would be committed and willing to continually fill my void with love and affirmation. In the process, I ended up pushing her away.

Despite clear memories of school from the age of four, I have nothing but fragments of memories at home until about age eight. I always thought I had such clear memories of my childhood because I could remember all the details of my house. I can clearly picture every room, every piece of furniture, the books in the bookcase and the pictures on the walls. But through the counseling, I realized that although I remembered details, I had almost no knowledge of experiences. I could never find myself as a child in the home, as I could in school. Part of that was because I had never *felt* happy at home. I never *felt* secure. I never *felt* wanted. Those are feelings of rejection.

Then my counselor showed me that some of the treatment and reactions in my home were inappropriate and were, in fact, an emotional form of sexual abuse. I was stunned to think that anything like that might have happened to me. But that could explain why I seem to have so much compassion for people who had sexual abuse in their childhood; why I am able to understand the problems it brings and identify it when the knowledge is suppressed; why I have the ability to comfort those who have been afflicted.

Rejection is the failure of parenting to provide the natural and necessary nurturing that is each child's birthright. *Sexual interference* or *abuse* is the disruption or distortion in God's design for the healthy development of the child's sexuality. These definitions are generalizations. Both come in many forms and affect people in different ways. Invariably, both leave long-term scars, and frequently open wounds that eventually must be brought to the Lord Jesus Christ for cleansing and healing.

The Only One Who Can Heal

I have never been more convinced than I am today that only by God's unique ability and supernatural power can any of us be healed of the adult manifestations of childhood trauma and dysfunction. Many hurting people spend years and countless dollars seeking help and healing from counselors, psychologists and psychiatrists, only to realize that they haven't been healed. They have been helped, but the ability to heal emotional wounds has never been given to man, any more than the ability to heal physical wounds has been given to a doctor. A doctor can help. He can lance the wound, he can cleanse it, he can treat it, but it has not been given unto him to heal it.

In the years that followed my counseling, God continued His amazing work of restoration in my life and emotions. The Scriptures tell me that as long as I am faithful He will continue that healing work in me:

> He who began a good work in you will perfect it until the day of Christ Jesus. . . . For it is God who is at work in you, both to will and to work for His good pleasure (Philippians 1:6; 2:13, NASB).

I know I am a new person. I know the healing work that the Lord Jesus has done in my life. The old feelings of rejection are gone, the old feelings of compulsions have been washed away by the healing power of Him who said, "I have come to heal the broken-hearted" (Luke 4:18; Isaiah 61:1).

"Something Different"

It is good to feel better about myself and know that God has been transforming me. My wife openly professes the changes she sees in me. At many different times, people have come up to me and said, "Fred, there is something different about you. What is it?" This is encouraging.

Just recently Florence and I were speaking at a church in Barrie, Ontario, Canada. On Saturday morning I was visiting with Donna Tripp. She said to me, "I saw you a little over a year ago when you and Florence were on '100 Huntley Street' for a week. But last night when I walked into the church and saw you again I couldn't believe you were the same person. There was such a difference. It was like love walked in. Your eyes were so much softer and gentler. When I saw you on television last year and looked at your eyes, at your whole countenance, I thought to myself, *There is something hidden there, something that isn't being revealed.* Everything you said was okay and I knew you were a Christian, but it was as if there was some kind of emptiness there. Boy, what a change!"

What have I done to achieve that change? Nothing more than abide in Him. By spending an hour or more daily in prayer and study, I am doing my part. He surely is doing His! He is still not finished with me. He who began a good work in me will continue to perfect what he started.

Florence and I are together virtually twenty-four hours a day, seven days a week—especially when we are traveling in ministry. People often ask us, "How many days a year are you away from home?" I answer, "Oh, about 250 to 275." That equates to almost nine full months in airplanes, hotels, churches; packing, unpacking and repacking; making connections, flying in and out of time zones, meeting with people and comforting those who are hurting.

And we love it! We enjoy it because we know this is what God has called us to. We know our lives are being used effectively to glorify Him, and we love it because we love each other and enjoy being together.

God has filled my life with His love, His joy and His presence. The old messages of rejection are gone. The bottomless pit has not just been covered over. It has not been bandaged. It is being filled daily to overflowing. Florence no longer feels compelled to try to fill that void. She can be herself. She no longer feels she is required to live up to my expectations. As I found release and freedom, Florence was able to experience it as well. She is no longer the secondary victim of my hurts.

After fourty-one years of marriage, we are more in love with each other than ever before. We now look forward expectantly to each new day and each additional year that the Lord gives us together. The present is so good longer think of the past years of heartache and frustration. I know they were there, but the pain is gone.

Complete freedom from emotional bondage and a new kind of life is not only possible, it is a promise of our Lord to all who call upon His name. I have experienced His promise of personal peace and restoration. I know He loves me. I know He died for me that I might have salvation, liberation and, ultimately, restoration. I know, also, that He loves you just as much. He died for you, no less than He died for me. Whatever pains, hurts or emotional bondage you may have experienced or endured, His promise is for you as well.

However, there is work involved; there is a journey you must take. His is a conditional promise; you have a role you must fulfill.

As Florence and I talk with troubled people, many say there is a wall between themselves and others—a wall that they don't know how to break down. Some picture themselves crouching behind a wall of fear. Some have built a wall of protection from the outside world. Some have walled up their emotions so they no longer feel their pain. Some have tried to knock the wall down by attacking it with anger. Some have tried to tunnel under the darkness in hopes they will come up on the other side of their pain. Some have wished for the wings of a dove so they could fly over their troubles into a sky of peace. Some have carved out a little hole in their wall and tried to peek through the chink in hopes of catching a sight of the promised land. Are you one of them?

We meet with women and men daily who are in emotional bondage, who are prisoners of past pains, who long for someone to break down the walls surrounding them and give them peace.

We must ask ourselves these questions:

- Do I have the desire to move from pain to peace? (If you do, this book will give you encouragement and hope.)
- Am I willing to follow God's directions—even if it means I will have to work through past hurts and dedicate some significant time to the Lord each day? (If you follow what Scripture tells you, you can be assured God's words will ultimately bring you to a place of peace.)
- Do I trust God with my life? (Some of us have been hurt by others and find it difficult to relate in a personal way with God. This book will help you take hold of the promise of healing and renew your trust in God.)
- Am I willing to praise God even though life has not been fair and times are not always joyful? (Remember, He says He inhabits our praise and our prayers.)
- When I get close to the promised peace and rest, will I reach out and possess the land? Will I take hold of the answers and be willing to move on to a healthy resolution of my emotional pain?

He has assigned to us a path to follow in our own journey to cleansing and healing: "Therefore, *having these promises,* beloved, let us *cleanse ourselves* from all *defilement of flesh and spirit*" (2 Corinthians 7:1, NASB).

4

"I NEVER FELT LOVED"

Dear Fred and Florence,

Feeling too shy to approach you after the seminar, I am writing this note to thank you and congratulate you for the insight, advice and spiritual leadership you gave so openly, humorously and professionally.

It was a poignant message for me and, I believe, many other people in the audience. The seminar was both a confrontation and an inspiration. I am at a stage in my life where I have removed the masks I have hidden behind for most of my twenty-nine years. I am gradually rebuilding the personality that is the me God intended. I am sure you understand how scary the journey is—although today I feel my path is more clearly marked by my growing faith in Jesus Christ. As I learn to trust Him, the trip is easier and better defined.

Early on in the journey, I was overwhelmed. Taking away the masks left nothing but a frightening void. I no longer had the energy or desire to keep wearing the masks, but the pain associated with their removal was equally harrowing. I was so accustomed to pleasing others and being what they wanted me to be, being strong, not weak (and hence hiding my emotions), that there was nothing of my self. Admitting I needed help was traumatic—it came in the form of a nervous breakdown three years ago and then another more severe breakdown and suicide attempt this year which hospitalized me in a psychiatric ward for four months.

Yet taking the risk to release the hurts that steamed to a boiling point inside me has made me a healthier person. I've learned some wounds need exposure, else they fester under a bandage. A seminar like yours is giving me the confidence to take responsibility and action on my problems—handing my trust to the Lord.

My problems, like many people's, are intertwined and complex. I was molested three times as a child, by relatives and a close friend I trusted. The latter was a female. This left me with homosexual doubts about myself, as well as all the guilt and dirtiness of the other occasions. I was a competitive swimmer of national rating for thirteen years which meant self-worth and parental love was often measured by *winning* the race, not merely competing. I had an eight-year battle with anorexia nervosa which in the last two years, much to my shame, turned to bulimia. I was in a financial crisis, lived in a de facto relationship and, therefore, in sin before God, and grieved over a miscarried pregnancy. I was unemployed, self-hating, lonely and harboring immense guilt. I was gripped, not by self-pity, but by sheer terror which showed itself in panic attacks where I thought I would die. After the crisis passed, I was left dazed for a day or two. In short, there wasn't a lot of fun!

Now I am relieved. I rallied the strength to acknowledge my problems and accept help rather than give in completely. I now know I can never be healed unless I put the "trash" out for the "collector" in whom I entrust my soul. Your input this weekend has consolidated my awakening and religious belief. I know I have much to learn and that the ground for me is still shaky. I want to trust more and open myself to God, for I believe there can always be a glimmer of light in darkness.

Thanks once again, and peace to you both.

Phyllis

We received this letter from Phyllis one week after we had spoken at a women's retreat for her church. Phyllis clearly expresses the sexual interference that was committed against her as a child. She also describes the subsequent feelings, emotions and symptoms. She states that her "problems are intertwined and complex."

There are two clear strands of pain that are related throughout her letter. The first is clearly the result of the molestation. The second is the rejection she felt at home, the low self-worth and the conditional parental approval. She never really felt loved. This strand led her to seek that love outside the home in relationships which led to guilt feelings.

Take a few moments now to read over her letter again. With a pen or a highlighter underline or highlight each symptom of interference and rejection you can find. Count how many you have identified. You will see the devastating effects of her childhood experiences and deprivation on Phyllis's adult life. You may also see yourself and some of your feelings and emotions in her letter.

The Pain of Rejection

Feelings of rejection and emotional deprivation inevitably accompany the adult symptoms of childhood interference. But the results of rejection alone, even when there has been no sexual interference, can often be equally damaging and devastating.

Our friend Stormie Omartian describes the devastating effects suffered by one girl who never knew childhood love or approval:

> When I was giving my testimony at a women's prison . . . one very timid, fragile-looking young girl came and confessed to me what had put her behind bars. Tracy told me her whole story about being born to a mother who didn't want or like her and frequently told her so. Her stepfather repeatedly and violently beat and raped her, constantly treating her with hatred and contempt. She grew up desperate for love.
>
> When she was fifteen, she became pregnant by a teenage boy. This enraged her mother so much that she threw Tracy out of the home. The boyfriend deserted her also, and there were no other family members or friends to turn to.

One night when she couldn't deal with the crying baby any longer, all the failure and rejection of a lifetime rose up in her with such force she went out of control. Grabbing a pillow, she held it over the baby's face until the crying stopped. By that time the baby was dead. This part of the story was horrifying enough, but what she revealed to me further was something I'll never forget because it was a brutally honest revelation of the bottom-line need in every human being.

Her exact words to me were, "When I was arrested and my picture appeared on the front page of the newspaper, I felt proud of it because I thought, *Now I am somebody.*"

I was appalled at the crime and shocked at Tracy's revelation, but my heart broke for Tracy as well as for the baby. How well I knew that anyone deprived of love as a child will desperately seek it everywhere and anywhere she can, no matter how bizarre or irrational the method.

Although food allows us to grow physically and education causes us to grow mentally, it takes love for us to grow emotionally. If we aren't nurtured with love, our emotions stay at a child's level. Even though our body is grown and our mind is developed, the childlike emotions within us will reach out and grab for any kind of love and acceptance we can get because they have never matured.

"Tracy," I said, looking directly at her, "I'm here to tell you that in the eyes of Jesus you have always been somebody.

"In the Bible it says before you were born the Lord saw your unformed body and planned all your days [Psalm 139:16]. He knows all about you [Psalm 56:8] and has chosen you [John 15:19] and loved you so much He died for you [John 3:16]. He has made you special [1 Corinthians 7:7] and has called you to be and do something wonderful for His purpose [2 Timothy 1:9]."

I never saw Tracy again after that weekend, but I have prayed for her often. She was a living example to me of how we all need love, recognition and acceptance. Thankfully in Jesus we can find all of this.[1]

Every one of us, to some degree, is a victim of rejection. Rejection is the result of the failure of parenting to provide necessary nurturing. Who has been raised by perfect parents? Obviously, no one. Most of us and our parents, though, did the very best we knew how. Our parenting is based on our own storehouse of lifetime learning, experiences and emotions. Some children grew up in a home where they truly felt loved. Many others felt lesser degrees of that love, to the point that, like Tracy, they never experienced any love at all. As a parent, Tracy had no solid foundation upon which to stand, resulting in a succession of poor choices.

Feeling Loved

When I meet with someone who has come to me for help, I often ask, "Did you feel loved as a child?" Although some answers are directly and flatly, "No," the most frequent response is, "I know my parents loved me."

Then I remind this person, "That was not the question I asked. Did you *feel* loved as a child?"

After pondering their feelings as a child for a few moments, the response is usually, "No, I don't think I really did feel loved."

Rejection is a deception, and the first step is to acknowledge its existence. Barbara Taylor, whose book *From Rejection to Acceptance* has helped many understand and cope with their feelings of being unloved, writes, "Until I was honest enough to admit there was a problem, I had no reason to seek help from God or man. More serious than this was the fact that until I saw the problem was with me, I was convinced that the whole world around me had the problem."[2]

Taylor also lists five lies that are planted in a child's mind, each one building on the other:

> "I am not loved."
> "I must be unworthy of love."

> "I must perform to win love."
>
> "If I cannot properly perform, I will be ultimately rejected."
>
> "If I am rejected, then I must compensate for this rejection."
>
> A pre-school child is basically without emotional defenses or understanding. That child has only one way to deal with feelings of rejection, and that is to try to bury them in his subconscious mind . . . though they may be temporarily forgotten, they will almost completely influence future behavior.[2]

Florence and I have seen that the adult manifestations of rejection are often very similar to those symptoms resulting from childhood interference. They are frequently intertwined, as Phyllis described in her letter. Likewise, the steps to cleansing and healing are the same.

Steps to Healing

First, I must acknowledge the fact that I have the symptoms of childhood rejection. This step is crucial for breaking the bands of bondage. Second, I must recognize who I am in Christ; that I am so loved that one man, the Son of God, the Lord Jesus Christ, was willing to surrender His life on that cruel cross for me. Third, I must participate in the ongoing process of cleansing and healing the hurts, the lies and the pains that were planted in me years before through coming daily to Him in prayer (we'll discuss this aspect in more detail in the section, "The Promise of Healing").

Some of you who are victims of rejection will be able to work through these three steps on your own, supporting them with diligent study and the regular reading of good books as resources to help you understand your emotions and reactions. There is no reason at all, however, for you to feel ashamed if you find you need help. Caring Christian counselors are trained to help you see, understand and replace the bottomless ache in your heart with the filling from the fountain of living waters. Do not hesitate to seek compassionate Christian help.

Fran, a woman in her fifties, remained in her seat after a recent seminar. After chatting with and giving encouragement to those who stood in line, I went over to Fran and sat down next to her. This beautiful and fashionably dressed Christian woman began to sob as she told me of all the pain of rejection from childhood that had a firm grip on her emotions. She asked me if I would have any time to see her. We made an appointment to meet while Florence was speaking the next morning.

From outside appearances it was inconceivable that this attractive woman had deep emotional hurts. I asked Fran to complete the simple survey we use to ascertain the nature of the hurts she was experiencing now or the trauma she may have been subject to as a child. (This survey form and its use is described in Part II, "The Promise of Knowing.") Of the forty-five symptoms listed, she only checked off seven. Three of these, however, were especially significant, and are described as "clear symptoms" of childhood sexual interference. They were "Feel unworthy of God's love," "Self-hatred," and "Uncontrollable crying." We then discussed questions that help us determine what types of physical sexual interference may have been committed against the adult as a child. Fran's responses to these questions were quite surprising. Despite the three clear symptoms indicated on the survey form, there was no clear evidence of the physical kind of sexual abuse.

Returning to the survey, I asked Fran, "Why do you feel unworthy of God's love?"

She replied, "I accepted Jesus at the age of six, but problems started when fear set in. As a child, I always thought He was mad at me."

Even though she was the oldest of three children, she always was made to feel inferior, and even now didn't have much regard for herself. "My brother and sister far outshine me. When I was at college I did all sorts of things to be noticed, to feel accepted. As a child, I always felt rejected. My mother said lots of mean things to me. She always made me feel I was clumsy and stupid. I can still clearly hear her words ringing in my ears, 'You'll never amount to anything. You're no good. You do nothing but cause me trouble.' "

I then asked Fran to tell me about the adult lives of her brother and sister, "What are they like emotionally today?" She described both of them as "a mess." Three adults, three lives in turmoil—all the result of a dysfunctional childhood family.

Fran went on to say, "I'm so ambivalent in my feelings. I feel like a chameleon. I don't know who I am." She remembers that when she was about eleven years old, "My father pulled down my panties and strapped me with a belt. My brother and sister heard it and I felt so humiliated. I think my father had a love-hate relationship with me. When I was about sixteen he told me of his unfilled sexual needs. He French-kissed me and fondled me. I felt mad, disgusted and affronted."

Fran had been in counseling for several years but never felt she had made much progress. I could not disagree, for her emotions were still raw and volatile. Fran never felt loved as a child. She never felt she was worth anything. She was able to see that she was clearly a victim of rejection. These and other things she related made it clear she was also a victim of the emotional kind of sexual abuse which damaged and distorted God's design for her healthy development.

We then discussed that it is not too late. The promise of restoration still applies to her.

Fran was emotionally deprived and discarded as a child—she never *felt* loved, valued or important. No one ever made her feel special. She was unable to accept God's love or to feel she was worthy of it. Much of her life was ruined by the parenting failure to provide the love and nurturing that every child needs. Her life can still be abundant as she comes daily to the Lord Jesus for His healing love. He alone can redeem the years that have been lost. He can give Fran purpose for the remainder of her life as she leanrs to encourage, minister to and comfort others who are hurting. He can still make something beautiful out of her life!

> Whosoever drinketh of the water that I shall give him, shall never thirst. . . . The water that I shall give him shall be . . . a well of water springing up into everlasting life (John 4:14).

Part II

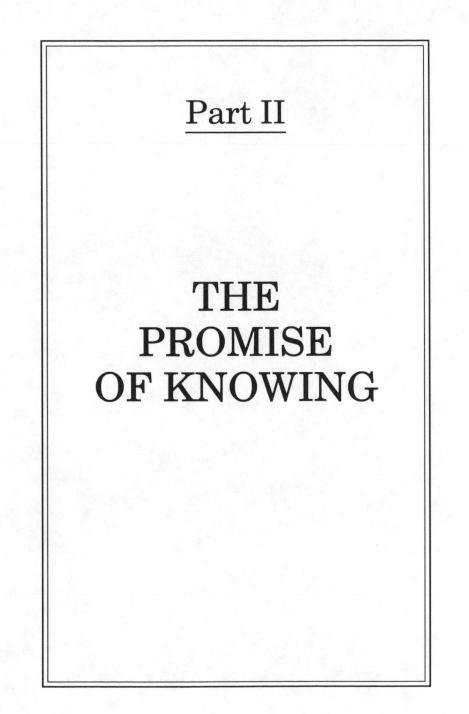

THE PROMISE OF KNOWING

5

TAKING OUT THE TRASH

In our town in Southern California some sophisticated councilmen voted to provide the citizens with custom-tailored trash cans. No longer would our streets have a hodgepodge of buckets and barrels. The decision was made without voter approval, and the "designer cans" arrived at each curb with the admonition that if we didn't use them the driver would not take away our trash.

Suddenly everyone was in an uproar. Did the council have the right to decide how we carried our trash to the curb? Could they dictate the dimensions of our buckets? Those who refused to conform to the designer cans found their trash left on the curb. A sense of insecurity wells up in a person whose trash isn't good enough to go to the dump.

For those of us who accepted the controversial containers, we felt a certain pride that our trash cans were above average, that we had classy trash. As a reward for our obedience to the ordinance we were guaranteed that a trash man with an automated truck would pick up our discards every Tuesday and Friday at no additional charge to our present refuse tax.

Soon the citizens settled into acceptance. If we would use our special trash cans and walk them to the curb, the trash man would empty them into his truck and take our trash away. As the system seemed to function flawlessly, my faith in the unseen trash man increased. Though I have never seen him come, I continue to believe in him because when I look into the big black containers, they are empty. The trash man comes silently in the night, removes my refuse and never brings it back. What a relief. I don't have to fear walking out the door one morning and finding my trash dumped in the driveway.

Yes, I have faith in my unseen trash man because he keeps his promise to come twice a week. But there is one prerequisite to his service. I have to walk my trash container to the curb. He doesn't knock on my door and ask me for my wastebaskets. I have to make the first move.

Often as we discuss with hurting people the need to dig up the trash of their past in order to be done with its influence on their present, someone will ask, "Isn't it better to leave well enough alone?" Our answer is, "If well enough is well enough, then by all means leave it alone. Don't try to fix something that isn't broken." If you have no symptoms, no undiagnosed aches, no pains and migraines, if your marriage is flourishing, if you have no outbursts of anger or feelings of rejection, if your career is promising, your finances are on solid footing, your personal relations are outstanding, and your children are rising up to call you blessed, then you have no reason to dig around in your past. But if you are often in physical or emotional pain and the bottom seems to be dropping out of your life, perhaps you need to open your own container, look inside and walk it to the curb.

First John 1:9 says: "If we confess our sins [take those things we've done wrong and the abuses that have been put upon us and bring them to our unseen trash man], he is faithful and just to forgive us our transgressions and to cleanse us [he is willing to empty the can and even wash it out] from all unrighteousness [anything dirty that we have done or that has been done to us at any time]."

Not only can we have faith that our unseen "trash man" will take all our trash away as He has promised, but He will never bring it back. Once we've given it to Him, He will never go back on His word.

Bonnie wrote to us after we helped her "take out her trash":

> My husband and I have been married thirty-three years and love each other very much, but I have worn so many masks—at home, in church, with friends. I don't really know who Bonnie is, but I want to. I believe I'm a sanguine but someone popped my bubble a long, long time ago. I thank God for Jesus Christ who doesn't try to repair old bubbles but gives us a new, clean heart and the truth that sets us free. When healed, I hope to be available to encourage others to put out their trash for God to collect and be free.

But we must first find out where our trash is, put it in our own container and walk it to the curb.

Scriptural Authority for Dealing With the Past

The more we study Scripture, the more we see that it not only applies to the sins we commit, but it also applies to the sins many of us have had committed against us—sins such as childhood emotional deprivation, rejection or childhood sexual interference. Any of these traumas inevitably result in various devastating manifestations in the child's adult life. In addition, further complications are added by emotional or physical abuse, alcoholism, divorce, an absent parent, a short-term surrogate parent, or any form of childhood instability.

Some of the most frequent adult evidences of these sins committed against the child are anger (controlled or expressed), long-term or continuing depression, low sense of self-worth, deeply rooted or excessive fears, sexual compulsions, marital struggles and feeling unworthy of God's love. (A complete list of possible symptoms can be found in the section "Additional Helps.")

The Lord tells us to "make the tree good, and its fruit good . . . for the tree is known by its fruit" (Matthew 12:33,

NASB). If we, the tree, are bearing fruit that is spoiled or unhealthy, it is time to take action.

The Lord chastised the Pharisees: "First clean the inside of the cup . . . so that the outside of it may become clean also" (Matthew 23:26, NASB). Because digging up the sin committed against us may be painful, many of us would prefer to ignore or cover it, mistakenly thinking, *If I leave it alone, maybe it will go away.* Proverbs 28:13, however, tells us that, "he that covereth his sins shall not prosper, but whoso confesseth . . . them shall have mercy."

First John 1:8,9 says, "If we say we have no sin [anger, for example, or a sin committed against us] we are deceiving ourselves, and the truth is not in us" (NASB). On the other hand, "If we confess [acknowledge or agree with God] our sins [including those committed against us], He is faithful and righteous to [first] forgive us our sins [those we commit], and [second] to cleanse us from *all* unrighteousness [those committed against us!]" (1 John 1:9). Looking back to verse 8, we see that "the blood of Jesus His Son, cleanses us from *all* sin," without limitation.

This passage clearly demonstrates one of the profound themes of Scripture: "If we . . . then He." *If we* confess our sins, *then He* cleanses. What is the requirement or prerequisite for us to receive His cleansing? We must do something. Effort or action is required of us. If we . . . then He!

At a luncheon following a recent conference, I asked a pastor of a large church if he felt it was necessary to dig up buried or suppressed sin or trauma in order to find cleansing and healing of emotional pain. I was surprised by his prompt reply, "Absolutely!"

If there is buried trauma or suppressed sin, it must be dug up and brought to the light in order that there may be cleansing and healing.

In the story of Achan in Joshua 7, "The Lord said unto Joshua . . . 'Israel hath sinned . . . they have even taken of the accursed thing . . . and . . . have put it even among their own stuff . . . neither will I be with you any more, except ye destroy the accursed thing from among you . . . *thou canst not stand before thine enemies* until ye take away the accursed thing from among you.'"

God's instructions for digging up the sin were swift and clear. There was to be no delay: "In the morning, therefore, ye shall . . . " It is a fascinating study to see, of all the tribes of Israel, how quickly God zeroed in on the offender, Achan, and how promptly Joshua acted: "So Joshua sent messengers, and they ran into the tent; and, behold, it was hid in his tent and the silver under it." And the sin, the sinner "and all that he had were destroyed."

Further confirmation can be found in Psalms: "Cleanse thou me from secret [hidden] faults" (19:12), and "Behold, thou desireth truth in the inward parts: and in the hidden part thou shalt make me to know wisdom" (51:6). Matthew 10:26 gives us the assurance that "there is nothing covered that will not be revealed, and hidden that will not be known" (NASB).

Even the parable of the tares and the wheat takes on a richer and deeper meaning when we associate it with the work of the enemy in the life of a child:

> The kingdom of heaven may be compared to a man [God] who sowed good seed [you and me] in his field. But while men [our guardians] were sleeping, his enemy [the devil, verse 39] came and sowed tares [interference, abuse] also among the wheat, and went away. But when the wheat sprang up [the child grew] and bore grain, then the tares [the results, symptoms] became evident also.
>
> And the slaves of the landowner [God] came and said to him, "Sir, did you not sow good seed in your field? How then does it have tares?" And he said to them, "An enemy has done this!" And the slaves said to him, "Do you want us, then, to go and gather them up?"
>
> But he said, "No, lest while you are gathering up the tares, you may root up the wheat with them. Allow both to grow together until the harvest [maturity]; and in the time

> of harvest I will say to the reapers, 'First gather up the tares; and bind them in bundles to burn them up'" (Matthew 13:24-30, NASB).

Not only can we see from this powerful passage of Scripture that we are to acknowledge the presence of the tares, but we also are to identify them for what they are. We are to gather them, bind them and burn them up. Not one of these truths of Scripture indicates that we should deny the existence of sins committed against us. On the contrary, except the chain be broken by acknowledgment, exposure, cleansing and healing, the sins of one generation are all too often passed on to the next, and the next, and the next.

If your childhood home was dysfunctional, examine the childhood homes of your two parents. You may be surprised to find similar characteristics in at least one, if not both. If you are able, learn what you can about the childhood experiences of your four grandparents. You may find that similar traits are there. If you were able to get information about the childhoods of your eight great-grandparents, it would not be surprising to see some of the same patterns there as well. If you are married, you might want to do similar research into your spouse's side of the family. Now is the time to break "the bands of your yoke and . . . go upright" (Leviticus 26:13).

Scriptural Authority for God's Healing

We believe the Scriptures clearly show that if there has been sin committed against us in our childhood, it needs to be uncovered and brought to the light. In addition, the Lord Jesus Christ Himself promises us we will know the truth about our past if we desire to know. And even if we are unwilling, God still wants to work in our lives: "God is always at work in you to make you willing and able to obey His own purpose" (Philippians 2:13, TEV).

Once we are willing, He declares emphatically in John 8:32, "Ye *shall* know the truth." And He will be the instrument to help us search for that truth.

Many of us have years of our childhood that have simply disappeared from conscious memory. We may look at family pictures and have no memory of them being taken, but there we are! Several years of life are simply gone. This is called a memory gap, a sure signal that something traumatic happened that caused those years to be lost. Once again our Lord, in the Scriptures, provides the plan for healing: "What woman having ten pieces of silver [years], if she lose one piece, doth not (1) *light* a candle, (2) *sweep the house,* and (3) *seek diligently* till she find it?" (Luke 15:8) "Therefore, beloved, since you look for these things, be diligent to be found by Him, in peace, spotless, and blameless" (2 Peter 3:14, NASB).

Knowing that we have a right to the truth, God assures us of His Guidance: "But the Helper, the Holy Spirit, whom the Father will send in My name, He will teach you *all* things, and bring to your remembrance *all* that I said to you" (John 14:26, NASB). It is the function of the Holy Spirit to bring all things to our remembrance. When our memory bank is like a strongbox, encased by heavy steel straps and secured by a big padlock, the Holy Spirit has the key. He is the key to opening it and bringing all things that are hidden into the light. An additional promise is given in John 16:13: "When He, the Spirit of truth, is come, He will guide you into *all* the truth."

We read in 1 Corinthians 2:10: "To us God revealed them through the Spirit; for the Spirit searches *all* things" (NASB). And in Jeremiah 17:10: "I the Lord *search* the heart, I try the reins, even to give every man according to his ways, and according to the fruit of his doings."

Hebrews 4:13-16 tells us:

> There is no creature [or experience] hidden from His sight, but *all* things are open and laid bare to the eyes of

> Him . . . since . . . we do not have a high priest who cannot sympathize with our weaknesses . . . Let us, therefore draw near with confidence to the throne of grace, that we may receive mercy, and may find grace [favor, spiritual strength] to help in time of need (NASB).

And finally, let the beautiful truth of this beatitude ring in your ears: "Blessed are those who hunger and thirst for righteousness, for they [and only they] shall be satisfied" (Matthew 5:6, NASB).

If there is trash in our house, in our home, in our life, in our emotions, we must gather it up and put it out at the curb for the trash man to take away once and for all. We cannot, however, take out the trash unless we see it, acknowledge it or find it. And for some of us, that which we have been treasuring is nothing more than trash!

Practical Application

If you are driving your car and it starts to sputter and miss, or it dies at the stop light or you start to hear funny noises in the engine, you know you have signs of internal problems. Do you ignore these symptoms and hope they will go away? Well, yes, sometimes we do just that, especially if we don't have the money for repairs.

A friend shared with me a humorous story about a woman who had to drive several hours to pick up her husband who was stranded with car trouble. As she drove, she heard strange noises from the front of her own automobile. By the time she arrived to rescue her husband, black smoke was pouring out from under the hood. He said to her, "What is all this smoke from?"

She said, "I don't know, but several miles back the car began making an irritating noise. I turned up the volume on the radio so I wouldn't have to listen to it." Her failure to pay attention to the warning signals had gotten them into even deeper trouble.

If our car isn't working right, we will eventually have to take it to an expert who can determine the cause of the problem and repair it. If there is a noise in the engine, it is not wise to open the hood and stuff a lot of cloth around the problem area in order to muffle the sound so we can feel better about driving the car. Such a measure is only temporary at best and will, more than likely, lead to even greater damage. We have to make the necessary repairs. So it is with emotional damage as well.

When Florence and I first met Betty, she was suffering from deep depression and had no idea where or when the pain had started. She couldn't remember a truly happy day. We encouraged her to look beneath the surface and try to find the source of her problems. In her search she has been to a therapist, in a support group, involved in a group therapy session with Incest Recovery Association and to a marriage counselor. We have personally encouraged her to keep hunting for the memories. She has listened to our tapes over and over and has thoroughly digested our book, *Freeing Your Mind From Memories That Bind.*

In her search she discovered that her grandfather, the only person she thought had ever loved her, had been the perpetrator. Through the years in which he was committing incest with her (before she was six years old), he was functioning as a church deacon, the church treasurer, and the director of the Junior Sunday school department. Finding the truth has been neither easy nor enjoyable, but Betty has finally taken her "car" in for the necessary repairs. Betty wrote to us:

> My road to recovery has been going on for over a year now, and it is emotionally draining but certainly worth all the effort I am putting into it. I am sick and tired of living the way I have been. I'm asking the Lord to "walk with me" through this recovery time and bring me out on the other side—whole, mature, complete in Him, living the abundant life which He has promised to all true Christians who

> surrender their lives to Him as Lord and Master. I think of you often when I need encouragement to continue this rough road to recovery. You are the first people who have given me any HOPE at all that I can survive the struggles in my life. Your encouragement and concern relit the candle of hope for me—a candle which was continually being snuffed out by depression, guilt, self-condemnation, self-hate, anger, bitterness and resentment.

Betty is traveling down the road to recovery with the promise of healing before her.

The Reality of Emotional Baggage

At one of our recent CLASS seminars, Patti asked if she could meet with me. We made an appointment for early one morning, just as soon as the conference started. As we met that morning, I apologized in advance to Patti that in a short while I would have to interrupt our meeting for about fifteen minutes as I was scheduled to speak on prayer. We then proceeded. Patti told me candidly of the many problems and issues in her life, most of which were symptoms of childhood sexual interference. Though her life was in turmoil, she could not remember any such interference happening in her childhood. I told her that it was possible to recapture lost memories, and that it was the function of the Holy Spirit to do that.

It wasn't long before I was told Florence would be ready for me in just a few minutes. I asked Patti to spend the time in prayer, asking God to unlock the suppressed memories of her past, laying a strong prayer foundation for the planned memory retrieval when I returned.

When I did return, Patti was eagerly waiting for me. There was a glow of excitement on her face. She had changed. She couldn't wait to tell me that while I was gone she had prayed just as I had suggested. During the time of prayer, the Lord revealed to her just as clearly as if it had happened yesterday the severe abuse perpetrated by her father when she was a very little girl. The Lord had retrieved a memory that had been totally suppressed. Instead of sobbing and trembling, Patti was glowing. At last she felt free—liberated from the bondage of her unknown past. Within those few minutes a transformation and her healing journey commenced. The Lord had literally set the captive free.

A few months later, I received this report from Patti:

> After studying many books on childhood abuses, I have found there are no areas in which I was spared. This includes emotional abuse, verbal abuse, physical abuse and sexual abuse, both personally and vicariously. My pastor made the statement, "Sanctified people who have excessive emotional baggage will struggle until the Holy Spirit frees them of that baggage," and I firmly believe that.
>
> I was four years old when the abuse started. I want you to realize that children don't ask questions. They just make their own conclusions. At four, I reasoned that if I weren't so pretty and bouncy and happy and delightful to hold, it wouldn't have happened. I took on a serious outlook toward life. In adulthood this mask displayed itself in anxiety, depression and an overall lack of trust.
>
> By the time I was seven I could rationalize the abuses in my seven-year-old mind. If only I hadn't cried, no one would have misused me. I quickly learned not to show my true feelings.
>
> The older I got, the more complex my reasoning became. I began to believe that if I could do everything perfect *and* make sure my younger sisters did everything perfect, all would change. This only led to tension, stress and more insecurity. I demanded perfection in all areas of my life and the lives of others.
>
> My last attempt at reasoning why this was happening to me was very futile but very real. During my adolescence, I believed that if only I had not been the oldest and if only I had not been a girl and if only I had not grown up, none of these things would have happened to me. These assump-

tions—these "if onlys"—led to anger, fear, guilt, self-hatred and total rejection.

All of this reasoning was done in my subconscious and just recently God has revealed it. I had no memories of my past—or so I thought. John 8:32 has become very real to me: "And you shall know the truth and the truth shall make you free."

My family was faithful to attend church. I was raised to respect God, especially under the hell-fire preaching that was so prevalent when I was a child. I gave my heart to God while in grade school and tried to please Him. I sat by my godly grandmother in church and watched her cry at every service. I just knew I would grow up to be as godly as she was. I rededicated my life as a teenager and always chose to live a good, acceptable, holy life. I lived it the best I knew how and yet, I could never get total victory.

I knew all the do's and don'ts of serving God and the church, and I followed them. So where was the joy? I was in the church every service, going to the altar for confession of any hidden sin, doing my share and more of volunteer work in the church, and yet, "sanctified people who have excessive emotional baggage will struggle until the Holy Spirit frees them of that baggage."

A couple of years ago during a revival, I once again went to the altar, but this time I returned to my pew a clean, whitewashed person. I knew it. After more than twenty years of searching, I had it. I was finally clean. Oh, the ecstasy of that moment is indescribable.

About this time Pam, the pastor's wife, taught "The Blessing." During this study she mentioned that we must make peace with our past. Since I had no memory of my childhood whatsoever, I asked her about just skipping that particular chapter. She said she could see an extreme amount of pain reflected in my eyes.

The Lord took over. By now I was willing to pay any price for the peace of God and that "white-washed" clean. I could feel it slipping away and I couldn't figure out why. Those old emotions of tension, anxiety, depression and "if onlys" were returning. I followed Pam's advice and began a study of my own past. Through your guidance and the

Holy Spirit, who shall "teach you all things and bring all things to your remembrance and guide you into all truth" (John 14:26,15:13), I began to see the extreme pain and continual abuse I had lived through. As the truth and the emotions surfaced, so did a hungering to be healed and freed. I wanted a new way to respond to myself and others and God. And I knew only God could heal and free a person from this emotional pain and excessive baggage.

Memory by memory, the Lord applied His touch until the emotional pain was healed. The memory remains to remind me of just how much Jesus loves me and cares for me—enough to take ALL of my pain upon Himself so I can be set free.

I can now serve God from a grateful, loving heart, not out of an incessant need to earn my salvation. Second Timothy 2:13 explains God's plan: "Even when we are too weak to have any faith left, he remains faithful to us and will help us, for he cannot disown us who are part of himself, and he will always carry out his promises to us" (TLB). I was weak and had very little faith because of my excess baggage. I had carried it for so long that I was near exhaustion physically, mentally and spiritually. However, the precious Holy Spirit took the truth of John 8:32 and set me free.

Freed in Christ,
Patti

* * * * *

List below some of the lies you have believed about yourself, such as:

1. No one loves me.
2. ______________________________
3. ______________________________
4. ______________________________
5. ______________________________
6. ______________________________

7. ______________________________
8. ______________________________

Now write the real truth about those lies, such as:

1. Jesus loves me. He died for me.
2. ______________________________
3. ______________________________
4. ______________________________
5. ______________________________
6. ______________________________
7. ______________________________
8. ______________________________

6

CHARACTERISTICS OF ADULT CHILDREN OF DYSFUNCTIONAL FAMILIES

For some of us, the emotional pain in our lives has become so much a part of us that we don't realize it is abnormal.

In recent years much has been written about adult children of alcoholics and their common misperceptions, attitudes and behaviors. Similar characteristics are evident in adults raised in dysfunctional families where the abuse was physical, emotional, verbal or sexual. In this chapter we will review sixteen adult symptoms which we have found to be common among adults who grew up in dysfunctional families. See if you recognize yourself among these symptoms.

1. Unhealthy Sense of Normal

Each of us has only our own environment in which to develop a standard of "normal" for behavior and lifestyle. If fighting was the norm in our home, we assume fighting is a norm in everyone's home and an acceptable standard for an adult lifestyle. If sexual or physical abuse occurred from the beginning of our conscious memory, we assume abuse is common in every home. Unfortunately, we tend to repeat the standards of our childhood home in our adult life, reproducing what may be an unhealthy family dynamic. We think we are functioning normally, but we are not. We simply have no experience with what is considered normal.

Florence and I have a friend who works with AIDS patients. As Gayle gets to know her patients, she frequently asks if they were molested as children. Generally, their initial answer is no. However, as Gayle gently explains what molestation really is, the patients often respond in surprise, "Those things happened to me as far back as I can remember, but I thought everybody did that. I didn't know that would be considered molestation or abuse."

2. Need for Control

Adults from dysfunctional families resist change and frequently exhibit a strong need for control. When they join a new group or start a new job they are likely to stir up dissension within their new environment in order to draw followers to themselves and be able to exert influence and correct things they perceive to be wrong.

Those of us who grew up in dysfunctional families had no control over what was done to us. We were at the mercy of manipulative and demanding parents and a troubled environment. Because of this tight control, as adults we tend to fear change which is forced upon us. If we are not in charge we feel we will once again lose control of our lives. We try to maintain a firm grip on things, not realizing there is something from our past motivating our reaction.

In marriage I had an unhealthy need for control. Underneath I was afraid I'd appear weak. Florence and the children learned to avoid bucking me for control and their avoidance of causing trouble fed my opinion of myself. I believed that I was not an angry person but a father who knew best.

3. Rigid Expectations

Those of us who grew up in overly controlling families tend to be very rigid in our personal expectations and in what we expect of our friends. Everything is black or white, all good or all bad. Each person is friend or foe. If a person disappoints us in any way, we often terminate the friendship immediately, claiming complete betrayal.

I had rigid expectations and insisted that my family meet them all. Although I felt I gave unconditional love, I would withdraw approval when performance was not what I desired. I believed I was setting high standards.

4. Fear of Failure

Children raised in a dysfunctional family often have difficulty following a project through from start to finish as adults. Some procrastinate and others never even begin. Although we don't consciously understand why we never seem to be able to get on with life, often our hesitation stems from our fear of failure. In some childhood homes, perfection was expected of even small children and nothing less was accepted. Yet no one ever seemed willing to take the time to show us how to plan and complete a project. We often had to guess at how to do the work assigned, and then we were left to wonder if it would be accepted. Some of us who didn't know what to do were too ashamed to ask for help. Habitual procrastination is frequently a sign of the fear of failure.

One woman shared with us that her father often promised to take her somewhere special, but as they were going out the door he would notice a dishtowel out of place or a rug wrinkled up. He would then announce they couldn't go because she hadn't done her work perfectly. No wonder the child was paralyzed into inaction.

5. Distorted Sense of Truth

Lying is basic to the dysfunctional family system. It can begin almost innocently when the child answers the phone and the parent says, “Tell her I’m not home.” The lies become a form of denial: denial of unpleasant realities, broken promises and inconsistencies. Reality is warped or perverted. The basic lie in dysfunctional families is. “We don’t have a problem—everything at home is okay.” The family rarely discusses truth openly with anyone, not even each other. This does not mean that in their own private thoughts each member doesn’t have some recognition of the truth, but they struggle to deny it and conform to the family lie.

Part of the lie is that the non-compulsive or non-addictive parent often covers up for the compulsive or addictive parent. The children observe this and learn to do it also. In some homes one parent blames the other for the neglect or abuse which is going on, but no one takes action. In the case of an absentee parent, usually the father, the mother frequently believes she is honor bound to excuse or cover for Dad.

Some of us can look back and see that lying served as a survival measure when we were small children. Denial of reality is often what kept us going. It helped us stand the life we had. Unfortunately, as we grew up denial often became a way of life, forming a destructive pattern that we don’t even realize exists. Often we are even proud of our integrity. Our sense of truth is fuzzy.

Although I prided myself on being scrupulously honest, I had an unrealistic view of myself and those around me. I believed all our family difficulties were someone else’s fault, denying the reality of my contribution to our problems. I was always quick to establish blame, therefore removing myself from responsibility. I could always give logical explanations that defied rebuttal, causing Florence and the children to give up in despair and let me win.

6. Low Self-Worth

Children who are constantly criticized and made to feel they are never good enough often come to believe they are terrible kids and their families would be better off without them. Their beliefs are often reinforced with such blaming accusations as, "If it weren't for you, I wouldn't have to drink . . . or work so hard . . . or stay away from home." Or, "If I hadn't had you, your father wouldn't have left. I never wanted you in the first place."

How many of us internalized similar criticisms and decided we were no good? Because there is no way to meet the perfectionist standards drilled into us from childhood, we see ourselves as always falling short of the mark. It is almost impossible for us to relax and tell ourselves, "It's okay just to be me." We always try to be good enough so someone will love us.

When I was a child and my grandparents came to visit, we were told how to behave and what to say. If we performed properly we were given a quarter. Although we didn't realize it, we were being taught that if you do and say the right things you are acceptable. Conversely, if we refused to kiss grandpa we didn't get money. When Florence and I were first married, I didn't think she expressed enough love, so I made her memorize a list of my virtues and recite them back to me. She was appalled at this phony lip service but it seemed only natural to me. As a child I had learned you could buy love and a feeling of worth, even if it was artificially motivated.

7. Finding Excuses

Those from dysfunctional families have a habit of blaming others. They criticize and judge, projecting their own real or imagined faults onto others to escape the condemnation they have heaped upon themselves. If you had parents who refused to take responsibility for their faults, you may have become the scapegoat. Perhaps your parents denied reality for their own survival, and were, therefore, unable to look at themselves realistically. They may have had many "shoulds" and "oughts" to live up to. Parents like this are apt to judge their children severely if the children don't come up to their parents' standards or expectations. Consequently, it becomes difficult for the children to have a normal, healthy relationship with their parents and others. They soon learn to do to others what had been done to them.

8. Personality Masks and Reactions

In her book *Your Personality Tree,*[1] Florence talks about *masking,* our tendency to function in a temperament which is not our natural, God-given personality. We have observed especially that the Sanguine child, fun-loving and carefree by nature, will often take on the Melancholy mask, a serious, sensitive personality. The Sanguine's fun has been buried under a pile of blame, guilt, anger and other forms of abuse. As this child matures, he or she fluctuates from flashes of humor to the depths of depression.

The Melancholy child, who already tends to take life seriously, may react to an abusive environment by giving in to a deep depression and may become suicidal. Every minor incident is a major trauma. Life is just too heavy to handle. He or she becomes a loner and retreats into a private world where emotions are suppressed and feelings seldom expressed.

The Choleric child of an abusive home determines to overcome and often becomes a compulsive worker and overachiever. His motto is, "I'll show them" which drives him to pursue perfection. The easy-going Phlegmatic tends to give up in the face of abuse and sigh, "What's the use?"

As a Melancholy I became a loner looking for perfection. If I could do everything perfectly maybe my mother would love me more and my father would notice my achievements. But no matter how I tried, my efforts brought no perceived love. The Choleric part of my nature then took over and I decided to show them. This desperate need for approval drove me to take foolish risks I should have avoided in my adult life.

According to our inborn personalities, we react differently to abuse or rejection and often cover our true nature with a mask.

9. Excessive Sensitivity

Those of us who can't laugh at our own mistakes or who feel hurt when others pick on us may well be repeating childhood feelings of rejection. If we were ridiculed as children, we expect to be ridiculed as adults. We will have a tendency to take everything that is said about us too seriously. We are often easily hurt by the ones we want to love us most.

For years I could not accept the things Florence said to me in humor. I had felt so rejected for so long that I expected to be hurt. I would be devastated by any casual remark she made. She eventually got so tired of my lack of humor that she stopped being herself and began to measure her words with me, causing us to have a somewhat artificial relationship. She could have fun outside of the home but when she was with me she had to guard her every statement. My sensitivity from childhood put a strain on our adult relationship.

Many of the adults we counsel have trouble having fun. They usually lack a sense of humor, and they often think people are laughing *at* them. They are overly sensitive whenever they think someone is talking about them and completely misinterpret positive things that are said to them.

10. Self-Righteousness

For those of us who come from dysfunctional families, life seems to be lived in an "all or nothing" mode. We appear to be very responsible but in reality we aren't. We will be loyal to a fault, but once we have become disenchanted with someone, it is unlikely that the relationship will ever be restored. We are as unforgiving as we were loyal. We tend to be impulsive in our behavior and even when we see we have made a wrong decision, it is extremely difficult for us to back down or admit it. Because we have not lived in a home where people were given room to fail or admit they were wrong, we may find it hard to forgive others whom we feel have wronged us. Because we have grown up in an environment of extreme denial, we easily feel that we are right and everyone else is wrong.

After I became a believing Christian, Florence told me I was so spiritual she couldn't stand me. Because of my childhood feelings of rejection, I had worked to make myself into the perfect person that I thought my parents would have loved. As I studied the Bible I measured myself by God's standards and felt I fulfilled all the laws. When I expressed disappointment in Florence's imperfections, I would quote her a Bible verse to prove to her that she not only displeased me but God as well. I became as self-righteous as the Pharisees and wondered why Florence couldn't see the love of the Lord in my life.

11. Shallow Relationships

Though they long for intimate relationships, adults raised in a stressful environment have great difficulty finding or establishing meaningful friendships. They have superficial relationships with others and often choose those who are having similar struggles. Abused women tend to be attracted to abusive men. An emotionally deprived person tends to bond with another person on a similar level of emotional pain. Victims tend to marry victims.

Some of us may be afraid of intimacy. We may fear losing control or we may not want to allow anyone inside our protective wall. Being emotionally mature is extremely difficult for those from a dysfunctional background for many reasons:

(1) We have no frame of reference for a healthy, intimate relationship. If our parents didn't model a healthy relationship, we probably aren't sure how one functions.

(2) We carry with us an inconsistent parent-child relationship. We received ambivalent messages of "Love me, love me not"; "Come close, go away"; or "Help me except when I don't want you to." The messages we received from our parents were neither clear nor consistent. We always had to guess at the meaning, trying to read the parent's mind.

(3) Our feelings of low self-worth cause us to believe we don't deserve a good relationship or a deep bonding in love. We seldom have a realistic sense of unconditional love.

(4) We fear being open to another person. What if they betray or hurt us as our parents did?

(5) Because of our lifetime of denial, we have never learned how to be open and honest about our feelings. We may not even know what feelings truly are.

12. Craving Approval

From the moment we are born we are crying for attention. As we begin to walk and talk, nothing means more to us than our parents' approval. If our parents nod and praise us, we perceive we are good. If they constantly nag and criticize, we feel we are bad. If the negative input outweighs the positive input, we grow up with an insatiable appetite for praise and will do almost anything to get it. One young woman I talked with had a father who told her she was ugly and would never get a man. She became promiscuous as a teenager and married the first man who asked her. A petite woman who came to a church seminar wearing a low-cut, provocative outfit later told me that her father had always told her only tall girls could be sexy. She was subconsciously trying to prove him wrong.

I remember how much I desired my father to come and watch me play sports. Because I craved his attention I participated in football, baseball, basketball, swimming, tennis and track; I also lettered and won medals. If I were the best, someone would have to notice. But no one did. The only time my father showed up was at a track meet—after I had run my race.

When I became the country club tennis champ as an adult, I wanted and expected Florence to watch every match. She didn't understand why, during one of my matches, I walked off the court and took away the *TIME* magazine I saw her reading and asked her to pay attention. Isn't it amazing that we often demand from our mates what we didn't get as children?

13. Socially Uncomfortable

So many of us who felt rejected as children feel we are different from other people. We assume that everyone but us is comfortable in social situations and that we are the only ones who feel anxious or awkward. We isolate ourselves and don't develop the social skills necessary to feel comfortable in a group. It is hard for us to believe that we could be accepted for who we are and that acceptance does not have to be earned. Feeling different, unwanted and insecure has become "normal" for some of us.

During my teen years I felt I was on the "outside." I often did strange things to attract attention and hopefully win friends. I remember a teen party where there was a pie-eating contest. We were to put our hands behind our backs and eat with our mouths, putting our faces into the pie. Instead of being a good sport I grabbed a fork off the table and began to eat daintily, thinking this would be humorous. The other kids just poked fun at me and I realized that I had made a fool of myself. So often I did the wrong thing in my desire to be accepted.

14. Unrealistic Sense of Ability

People who grew up in dysfunctional homes where deception and denial went hand in hand have no honest way of evaluating themselves or their abilities. On some days their behavior would be acceptable while at other times the same action would bring parental wrath.

Those of us who tried to please demanding parents were always doing more and more, sometimes taking on a task without first counting the cost. No one took time to help us decide if we were apt to fail or succeed. We didn't know how to evaluate whether we had the resources or abilities. Sometimes we reached the point where we could see that we could never please them. Our families failed to value each others' talents, causing us to develop an unrealistic sense of our own capacities.

As I look back, I realize I had no guidance in career choice. It was expected in our family that the children would go to college and I am grateful that my parents provided for us. However, there was no time spent evaluating what aptitudes we had for what vocation. I attended New York University where I majored in business. After graduation I apprenticed at Stouffer's restaurants, becoming an assistant manager. As I look back I realize my talents and abilities would have been better used as a lawyer and I have many times regretted that I did not even think of the legal profession.

When I went into my own restaurant business I was never satisfied and kept opening more and more units, trying to show that I could be successful. My feelings of rejection and low self-worth made me stretch beyond what should have satisfied me until I ultimately lost much of what I had built. I had no honest way of evaluating my mental or emotional abilities and I caused my family much pain by not being able to see my weaknesses.

15. Irrational Loyalty

A dysfunctional home may very well have the appearance of being loyal, comfortable and tolerant. Family members will seem to be supportive of each other and will stand together long after reality and reason would objectively reveal unhealthy patterns. The apparent loyalty may be more the result of insecurity or fear of rejection than a healthy loyalty founded on genuine respect for each other. As the children grow up and go their separate directions, this artificial glue of loyalty disintegrates, and the true nature of the relationships becomes obvious—the siblings usually have little to do with each other. Unfortunately, the new generation of adults tends to replicate the same artificial relationships in their own homes.

Once my parents were both gone there seemed to be nothing to bring my brothers and sister and me together. Today our communication is infrequent, although basically cordial. In contrast, Florence's family has remained close. They keep in touch, can talk honestly with each other and are supportive in attendance at each others' family activities.

The dysfunctional family often talks of love and support but seldom lives it in the heart. They will either run from the home at the first chance or settle into a sick dependency that keeps them bound to Mother or Father forever.

16. Impulsive Behavior

Some of us seem to plunge from problem to trauma to disaster and never understand why. We don't realize that impulsive behavior is often part of the dysfunctional family.

We tend to move without seeing the alternatives. We tend to lock ourselves into a course of action without giving serious consideration to possible consequences. Our impulsiveness often leads to confusion, self-blame and loss of control. In addition, we are apt to spend an excessive amount of energy straightening out the mess we have created through our impulsive decisions.

Generally we do not have any conscious awareness of our actions. Whatever idea enters our head is put into practice. Once the pattern is begun, we don't seem able to stop. As our poor choices become compulsive, we rationalize why these things happened in order to excuse our behavior.

I believe that one of the reasons for this childlike impulsiveness is many of us feel we missed out on our childhood. Many children become a surrogate spouse in place of their dysfunctional parent or a caretaker for their needy siblings. Some of our present impulsive behavior may come from an unconscious wish to reward ourselves, treating ourselves like the little child we never got to be.

As I grew up, I established a pattern of impulsive behavior that has caused me and my family much grief. I stepped into business deals without sufficient investigation and always hoped it all would turn out right. Many times it didn't and I had to suffer the consequences.

Have you been able to identify any of these traits in your life or in the life of a friend—or your mate? If you were raised in a home where there was any form of interference in God's design for healthy development, you will probably exhibit at least one of these symptoms in your adult emotions and relationships.

Each of these behavior characteristics can be corrected if we are willing to admit that they do exist in our emotional makeup and if we have a desire to bring about change. Unfortunately, all too often we have no desire to acknowledge our symptoms. It is those who live with us who are hoping (and pleading) for changes.

As adults, if we can get beyond the denial of problems to an acceptance of their existence, we can then begin to identify the source of the problems. Then the healing work of the Lord can proceed.

If these patterns are a result of sins committed against us as children in the form of abuse or interference, Scripture makes clear that this kind of sin must be dug out, not ignored or glossed over. Sometimes it will be necessary to enlist the assistance of a competent counselor to recognize the existence of these symptoms, identify their roots and proceed with the restoration. But, it is only the Lord Jesus Christ who can heal.

As you proceed through this book, you will learn how to do your part in coming to Him for that healing.

> Come to me all who are weary and heavy laden, and I will give you rest. Take my yoke upon you, and learn from Me . . . and you shall find rest for your souls (Matthew 11:28,29, NASB).

7

ASTOUNDING RESULTS

Even before our book *Freeing Your Mind From Memories That Bind* was released, Florence and I had realized that many, many people with whom we spoke were totally unaware of any form of sexual interference in their childhood. (As I'll share later, I was one of them.) Some vehemently deny the possibility.

What was so significant, however, was that they seemed to have the same symptoms in their adult life as those who were aware and acknowledged victimization, molestation or other forms of abuse. They were having the very same struggles, but had no idea why. There was clearly an important correlation.

Early on we could see the significance of memory gaps in childhood, where periods or even years seemed to be blank. A large part of the workbook section in *Freeing Your Mind* is specifically designed to help the readers identify the age of their earliest memories and any later periods where memories are blank, and then to determine why those periods of life may be lost from recall.

We began to wonder how many men and women have so suppressed childhood trauma that they truly have no knowledge of it. Professionals who regularly deal with victims of childhood trauma believe that 25 percent of all women and 8 to 10 percent of all men had sexual interference or abuse of some form in their childhood. It is important to note that these figures reflect only those who acknowledge or are aware of the inappropriate activity.

What about the others who have similar or even identical adult manifestations but have no awareness or knowledge? How many of them are there?

In January 1989, we conducted a comprehensive survey to try to find the answers to those questions. The results of the first survey were so startling, we repeated the survey for the next ten weeks at thirteen Christian conferences. The conferences were held in churches, among conservative evangelical Christians, and on the campuses of two coed Bible colleges. During this time, a total of 2,465 of our prepared forms were turned in.

The survey form, reproduced here in its entirety, was completely "blind." (The dots that appear here did not appear on our survey and will be explained later.) At each conference, the participants were simply told we were conducting a research project and would very much appreciate it if they would take just a few moments to complete the form. No information was given as to the nature of the form or purpose of the project. We simply solicited their assistance. The percentage of survey forms returned at each conference varied from 40 to 70 percent.

This was an unusually high response for a group survey and can be attributed to a relatively captive audience. Since no one had any idea of the survey's nature, those forms not turned in can be attributed to people not wanting to bother, unwilling to express confidential feelings, or forgetting to complete the form or turn it in. The range of ages responding, except at the two Bible colleges, was predominantly age thirty to sixty. The ratio of women to men was approximately four to one.

SURVEY OF EMOTIONS AND EXPERIENCES

Your Status: Please Check All That Apply

Single ❑ Married ❑ Separated ❑ Age _____

Divorced ❑ Remarried ❑ Male ❑ Female ❑

Sanguine ❑ Choleric ❑ Melancholy ❑ Phlegmatic ❑

PLEASE CHECK EACH BOX THAT APPLIES OR EVER HAS APPLIED
(LEAVE BLANK ANY THAT DO NOT APPLY
OR YOU ARE NOT SURE OF)

	Father	Mother	You	Spouse
Abortion	❑	❑	❑	❑
Affairs during marriage	❑	❑	❑	❑
Alcoholic excess	❑	❑	❑	❑
Athesma	❑	❑	❑	❑
Childhood depression	❑	❑	❑	❑
•• Compulsions	❑	❑	❑	❑
•• Downcast looks	❑	❑	❑	❑
•• Eating disorders	❑	❑	❑	❑
Emotionally abused as child	❑	❑	❑	❑
Emotions suppressed in childhood	❑	❑	❑	❑
•• Fear of being alone	❑	❑	❑	❑
•• Fear of losing weight	❑	❑	❑	❑
• Feel unworthy of God's love	❑	❑	❑	❑
• Feel "dirty"	❑	❑	❑	❑
• Fits of rage	❑	❑	❑	❑
Guilt feelings	❑	❑	❑	❑
Hide real feelings	❑	❑	❑	❑
• Lack of resistance to sexual attack	❑	❑	❑	❑
•• Lack of trust	❑	❑	❑	❑
Low self-worth	❑	❑	❑	❑
Marital sexual disinterest	❑	❑	❑	❑
• Memory gaps in childhood	❑	❑	❑	❑
•• Migraine headaches	❑	❑	❑	❑
Mood swings	❑	❑	❑	❑
Nudity forbidden in childhood home	❑	❑	❑	❑
Obsessive fear of rape	❑	❑	❑	❑
Physically abused as child	❑	❑	❑	❑
•• PMS	❑	❑	❑	❑
Poor teenage opposite-sex relationships	❑	❑	❑	❑

Pornography in childhood home	❑	❑	❑	❑
Recurring bad dreams	❑	❑	❑	❑
Rejection feelings	❑	❑	❑	❑
• Same-sex attraction	❑	❑	❑	❑
• Self-hatred	❑	❑	❑	❑
Sexually abused or molested as child	❑	❑	❑	❑
Suicidal feelings	❑	❑	❑	❑
Teenage promiscuity	❑	❑	❑	❑
Tendency to overreact	❑	❑	❑	❑
• Uncomfortable with nudity in marriage	❑	❑	❑	❑
•• Uncontrollable anger	❑	❑	❑	❑
•• Undiagnosed pains, aches	❑	❑	❑	❑
TOTALS	______	______	______	______

❑ I have never been in counseling.

❑ I have been in counseling for ______ months or ______ years.

Type: ❑ psychiatric ❑ psychological
❑ pastoral ❑ marriage & family

❑ The counseling did help me.

❑ The counseling did not particularly help me.

❑ We did get to the roots of my problems.

❑ We did not get to the roots of my problems.

The surveys submitted at each conference were individually reviewed, totaled and evaluated. Conferences were local and national in nature and held in different parts of the country, giving a broad geographical base.

Of the 2,465 respondents, 2,002 were women. Of the women, 347 were students, mostly between the ages of eighteen and twenty-five. The other 1,655 women were non-students and predominantly thirty to sixty years of age.

The number of men responding to the survey was 463, of which 201 were students and 262 non-students. Age categories for the men were similar to those for the women. For clarification purposes only, the two groups will hereafter be referred to as students and adults. (This in no way implies that the students were not also adults.)

What the respondents to the survey did not know was that each of the forty-one emotions and experiences, except one, was an adult symptom of childhood sexual interference. The one exception: "Sexually abused or molested as a child." The list was carefully worded to allay any suspicion or guessing as to its nature. At some conferences, due to the content of the presentation, the true nature of the survey was later explained to those participating.

Of the forty actual symptoms, nine are what we term "clear symptoms." In our experience, these result almost invariably from childhood trauma. On the survey form the "clear symptoms" are indicated with a single dot to the left of the list. The acknowledgment of only one of these clear symptoms is a strong signal. The checking off of a number of these one-dot symptoms more clearly confirms the conclusion. Those items shown with two dots are described as "strong symptoms." The source of these symptoms could possibly be traced elsewhere. Nevertheless, they are regularly and frequently seen in adult victims.

The remaining symptoms, those without any dots, are described as "possible symptoms." They are considered to be less significant, having a greater number of possible roots.

A clear example of a "possible symptom" would be the first symptom on the list: abortion. Women have abortions because they are pregnant and do not wish to be (for a number of reasons), not because of childhood trauma. However, according to results of this survey, the group of women who acknowledge sexual abuse or molestation have three times as many abortions as those to whom no abuse is attributed. Therefore, abortion is not a "clear symptom" or a "strong symptom," but it does have significance as a "possible symptom." The number of these possible symptoms checked off, as well as clear symptoms and strong symptoms, further weights the conclusion and the evaluation of the individual's response.

The original purpose of the survey was simply to determine what percentage of Christian adults, without any prior knowledge of childhood interference, have the same or similar key symptoms as those who do have such knowledge. In other words, what percentage may have experienced such trauma, but have no awareness? The secondary purpose would then be to enable hurting Christians with no known reason or source for their emotional or physical pain to identify the cause, to be set free and, ultimately, cleansed and healed.

The first significant conclusion revealed by the survey was that the generally accepted percentages of men and women suffering trauma in their childhood were borne out. Of the adult Christian women attending our conferences, 387 of the 1,655 did check off "Sexually abused or molested as a child," which is 23.4 percent. Of the adult men, twenty-nine of 262 acknowledged abuse, or 11.1 percent. Startlingly similar to the figures estimated for the secular world.

The next category in our survey included those people who checked off only a small number of symptoms on the total list and checked none of the clear symptoms. They have probably lived a life relatively free of turmoil and emotional stress. This group was labeled "No sexual interference." There was no apparent evidence of childhood sexual trauma in their responses. It does not conclusively indicate that there wasn't any, but if there was it simply did not appear.

In evaluating each individual's response, a conscious effort was made to be certain that if an error was to be made, it was to be on the conservative side. If, in carefully looking over the form, there was a question as to the possibility of abuse, it was most often put into the "No sexual interference" category.

The third major group, comprising one-half of each of the adult women's and men's groups, have been classified as "Yes—Suppressed." In each of these responses the individual did not check off "Sexually abused or molested as a child," clearly indicating that they have no knowledge of such trauma in their childhood or, as may be the case for a few, they have knowledge of a "minor incident" in their childhood but do not consider it significant.

What is very significant for this group, 51.5 percent of adult women and 54.6 percent of adult men, is that they did acknowledge most of the same symptoms, or a similar number of symptoms, or at least one of the clear, one-dot symptoms (and in almost all cases, several) as those who acknowledged sexual abuse. We may conclude, then, that this large group, comprising half of all men and women attending these various Christian conferences may, in fact, have some form of interference in their childhood, but are unaware of it.

Combining these figures, the "Yes—Acknowledged" and "Yes—Suppressed," the survey indicates that an astonishing 75 percent of these adult Christian women and 65 percent of these adult Christian men have manifestations which are now affecting them, or have at sometime in their life.

One final note: Any such survey effort is subject to generalizations, the understanding by the respondent of the writer's intent, making rapid decisions ("Did it ever apply to me?") and a certain margin of error. These factors have been, as accurately as possible, taken into consideration.

SUMMARY OF RESPONDENTS
SURVEY OF EMOTIONS AND EXPERIENCES
JANUARY—MARCH 1989

	Apparently No Childhood Trauma	Acknowledged: Yes—Childhood Trauma	Evaluated: Yes—Trauma Suppressed	Totals
WOMEN				
Adult	381 (23.0%)	387 (23.4%)	852 (51.5%)	*1,655
Student	156 (45.0%)	44 (12.7%)	147 (42.4%)	347
TOTAL	507 (26.8%)	431 (21.6%)	999 (50.0%)	2,002
MEN				
Adult	90 (34.3%)	29 (11.1%)	143 (54.6%)	262
Student	124 (61.7%)	7 (3.5%)	70 (34.8%)	201
TOTAL	214 (46.0%)	36 (8.0%)	213 (46.0%)	463

*Includes 35 surveys marked "?"

Significance of "Clear Symptoms"

We'll now take a look at the one-dot symptoms and discuss why these symptoms qualify as clear indicators of childhood interference.

1. Lack of Resistance to Sexual Attack

Children are born with natural and healthy defense mechanisms. When those defenses are lacking in an adult, we strongly suspect some form of childhood abuse has weakened or destroyed them.

In counseling hundreds of women, Florence and I have found an amazing correlation. Women who indicated a lack of resistance to sexual attack had also been victimized earlier in life. The survey later bore this out.

Without the proper defense mechanisms, the victim of a sexual attack is often worn down emotionally by the persistence, ardor or demands of the abuser. She may be coerced or threatened, but the abuse is usually not violent. Though she does not want the experience, though she protests and even tries to protect herself, she ultimately accepts the intrusion because emotionally she feels she cannot win. It is as though her hands are tied behind her back. Seemingly, there are no defenses available to her. This type of violation is sometimes referred to as "date rape" and should not be confused with a traumatic "attack rape."

Victimization as a child can plant in a woman's emotions the idea she cannot win. She has been programmed to quit, to lose or to acquiesce. And even in the case of something as horrible as sexual attack, she reacts in the way she's been taught.

Lack of resistance to sexual attack is often a significant, clear symptom of childhood interference. A woman's determination, strength and ability to defend herself have been stolen away by a childhood trauma.

2. Obsessive Fear of Rape

No woman wants to be raped. No woman will knowingly put herself in a place or position where she might be in danger of attack. But not every woman has an obsessive fear of being raped every time she leaves the house, walks down a street or walks into an unknown public building.

Yet some women do have very real and intense fears. The reason is not simply a fear of the unknown. Even though there may be no present knowledge of it, the source of the fear is very likely a childhood traumatic experience; an unknown, locked-away memory which triggers adult reactions and obsessive fears.

In *Freeing Your Mind From Memories That Bind*, Florence and I share the story of a friend named Patti. Among the many severe adult manifestations she experienced were sudden uncontrollable anger, panic attacks, fear of being alone at night, severe PMS and an intense fear of rape. As Patti became willing to face these issues and prayed for the Holy Spirit to reveal the sources, she experienced five separate flashbacks of sexual abuse when she was about three years old by her mother and grandfather. Before this, the first six years of her life had been a total blank. As Patti brought these pains to the Lord for cleansing and healing, her symptoms gradually disappeared. I remember her telling me several months later that she had gone down to the Greyhound bus terminal to pick up a friend. She realized she had gone into the terminal, met her friend and never once even given a thought to the possibility of rape. Previously she would have been petrified to enter such a facility, so intense and present was her fear of rape.

3. Feel Unworthy of God's Love

Intellectually, Christians understand salvation. They know in their minds that they have received forgiveness of sins. Many adults who for years have known Jesus as Savior, and striven to live a holy and righteous life for Him, *feel* that they are failures, that they are not worthy of His gift of life. They *feel* guilty, ashamed or dirty, simply not good enough. They don't *feel* they will ever be able to measure up to what is expected of them.

Once again, we must ask "Why?" God created us in His image to have a hunger and natural affinity for Himself. That is part of our birthright. Why, then, have so many lost what is their right? We believe the answer lies in the destruction resulting from childhood sexual devastation. The feelings of guilt, shame and unworthiness are real, but they are lies, planted there by the father of lies, flourishing for years and continually wrapping more and larger bands of bondage around the adult.

Christine, a victim, wrote:

> I try so hard to establish an intimate relationship with the Lord, but I can't seem to get anywhere. I know I must love Him because I try so hard to please Him. He said those who love Me keep My commandments, but there is something missing or I wouldn't suffer from all this loneliness. I want Him to be *all* I need, just Him. I want to be what

He has in mind for me to be. These emotional problems are keeping me from being all that I can be for Him.

We have found that feeling unworthy of God's love is one of the clearest signs that something may have happened in childhood to rob you of that which God gave you as a birthright—the ability to enjoy your oneness with Him.

4. Feeling Dirty

When God's design for a child's healthy development has been distorted, he or she may feel dirty inside and out. It is an emotional feeling that no amount of intellectual rationalizing can wash away. If a child's body has been defiled, it is only natural that he will feel ashamed, guilty and unclean. Even when the traumatic experiences are totally blocked from conscious memory in adult life, the emotional feelings remain. Many women have underlying feelings of being dirty and have no idea why, or how to get free or clean.

5. Fits of Rage

Hurting people frequently express frustration over their inability to understand and control sudden outbursts of anger. These eruptions often are stirred up by some relatively inconsequential word or experience: a husband coming home ten minutes later than he said he would, a child spilling a glass of milk, a word that actually was spoken without any malice. Why? What causes a person to react so violently? Is there something buried deep inside that suddenly bursts forth when the fuse is ignited? Countless Christians continually struggle with this problem, despite sincere efforts to find relief, forgiveness and healing through counseling, prayer and Bible study.

Where does this explosive rage come from? Surely God did not instill this in us when He created us in His image. Surely this is not a fruit of the Spirit. For many years I thought my anger was simply an evidence of "sin in my life," the solution being confession and forgiveness. In this context, it could well be the result of sin in your life, but not sin that you committed. Rather, anger can be the result of sin that was committed against you. We know of no other consistent source of this clear symptom—adult fits of rage—than childhood sexual interference. The intense hurt, often totally unknown, is deeply buried in a boiling cauldron of explosive emotions.

6. Memory Gaps

Psychologists call memory gaps "traumatic amnesia," the loss of conscious memory of specific periods of life. We cannot remember every day, every experience, every emotion or word of our childhood. However, people who have not experienced abusive trauma in childhood generally have very clear and specific memories well into their earliest years.

In *Freeing Your Mind From Memories That Bind,* a section of the workbook portion enables the reader to return to his or her childhood years at home and school and recall his relationships. Many have found substantial gaps in their memory, as many as two or three years. It is not unusual for both men and women to tell us they have no memory whatsoever until ten or twelve years of age. They think this is normal until they talk with a friend whose clear memories begin at two or earlier.

Once again we must ask "Why?" What might have happened in someone's childhood to totally obliterate those years from conscious memory?

Florence talked to a hurting woman recently who acknowledged many of these symptoms of childhood interference, including no memory of her life between the ages of nine and twelve. She could remember her first nine years quite clearly. Then there was a three-year blank. Why were those years missing? She went to school. She played, had friends, slept, ate, experienced life. Where did those years go?

Florence asked her, "What happened when you were nine?"

"My mother died."

"Did anything happen that you can remember when you were twelve?"

"My father died."

The immediate conclusion might be that she experienced severe grief over the loss of her mother. But why would her memories recommence at her father's death?

Florence sensed there was more to the story. "Can you think of anything significant that happened after your mother died?" she asked.

"Well, all I remember is that on the night of the funeral, my father moved me into his room and I slept with him from then on."

In a few short moments, by knowing where to look and what questions to ask, Florence uncovered the source of most of this woman's adult hurts and pains, the manifestations of childhood trauma, and the reason for the memory gap of three years: This woman had apparently become her father's surrogate wife.

7. Same-Sex Attraction

When any man or woman has physical feelings toward a person of the same sex, has fantasies about such a relationship or has had actual experiences, the reason is often rooted in childhood interference with God's design for healthy sexual development of the child. People who are homosexual will vehemently proclaim, "You don't understand. I was born this way!" We do not believe this is true. The Bible clearly says:

> God created man in His own image, in the image of God created He them, male and female created He them . . . And God saw *everything* that He had made, and behold it was very good (Genesis 1:27,31).

In Leviticus 18, any aberration of appropriate sexual behavior is proclaimed an abomination. In verses 22 and 26, we read: "Thou shalt not lie with mankind, as with womankind: it is an abomination. . . . Ye shall therefore keep my statutes and my judgments, and shall not commit any of these abominations."

Could God have created man or woman in His image and likeness, deeming them to be good, and at the same time declare them an abomination? No. Scripture clearly teaches that God created us to be healthy and whole. It is Satan who interfered with God's plan. Further, in every man or woman with whom we have met who have homosexual tendencies, we have always found evidence of childhood sexual interference, or a preponderance of other clear symptoms.

We are aware that there may be some—especially young men and teens—whose lives have been filled with rejection and emotional abandonment, who have been seduced into homosexuality by an older, trusted figure. The question would still need to be answered: Were there additional childhood experiences that caused them to be vulnerable?

This is not an obscure problem in the church. Numerous individuals with whom we have personally met have confided that they face this battle. They fight and fight and often despair of ever gaining freedom from this form of bondage.

8. Self-Hatred

Does not the Lord command us to "Love thy neighbor as *thyself*" and "Let every one of you love his wife as *himself*"? Could God have created us to love ourselves and at the same time hate ourselves?

Many Christians, created by God and born again into His forever family, do hate themselves. They will fully acknowledge it if you ask. Seeds of self-hatred have been planted by the enemy among the good seeds planted by the Lord. They sprout, grow up and mature as tares among the wheat. The parable teaches us they must be gathered up, bound into bundles and burned. The lie must be destroyed.

God did not create us to hate ourselves, to loathe our bodies or to think there is nothing good in us. Self-hatred is a direct result of interference in the healthy sexual growth planned for us by our Lord.

9. Uncomfortable With Nudity in Marriage

When considering this symptom and expressing why they feel uncomfortable, women especially say things such as, "Well, I'm too fat"; or "I'm too thin"; or "I have too much here," or "not enough there." They are too embarrassed for their spouse to see their body, so they undress in the dark, in the closet or in the bathroom. If weight or shape are the real reasons for feelings of discomfort, why are so many other similarly proportioned persons perfectly comfortable?

Once again, the Scriptures specifically tell us we are to love our own bodies (Ephesians 5:28,33). God gave us the right and the ability to do that. If we cannot, then the answer must be that someone stole that birthright away from us. In our experience we have seen no valid or applicable cause other than childhood interference.

8

OTHER SIGNIFICANT FINDINGS

We decided to do some additional analysis on four "strong symptoms." (Because of various limitations, these studies have only been completed on a select list of symptoms submitted by women only.) You may be surprised by what we discovered.

1. PMS

We have long suspected that there is a significant connection with the presence of pre-menstrual syndrome and people with known or suppressed interference. The findings of the survey clearly confirm this correlation and further strengthen the premise that treating PMS symptoms with drugs will not heal the individual if the root cause is emotional and physiological stress resulting from childhood sexual interference. When the spiritual healing of that root cause takes place, the PMS symptoms can be healed, not just controlled.

From four different samples totaling 226 "Yes—Acknowledged" responses, 107 (47 percent) indicated problems with PMS. Of those in the same samples who were evaluated to have had no childhood interference, the figure was dramatically lower—only sixty-four of a total of 277 (12.3 percent).

Nearly one-half of the women surveyed who were known victims of sexual interference suffered from PMS, and approximately four times as many women who were violated suffered from PMS than those who were not.

One other significant finding was noted among those evaluated as "Yes—Suppressed." Of the total 545 responses, 229 (42 percent) indicated PMS problems. The 42 percent of the "Yes—Suppressed" sample groups is surprisingly similar to the 47 percent of the total "Yes—Acknowledged" groups.

This leads us to believe that pre-menstrual syndrome, while not considered to be a "clear symptom" can be considered a "strong symptom" of childhood sexual interference.

2. Migraine Headaches

Similar findings were found in the sample groups for those women who suffer from migraine headaches:

No sexual interference	9.1%
Yes—Acknowledged	27.3%
Yes—Suppressed	27.0%

Migraine headaches often have physiological causes. But far more frequently the basic underlying factor, as seen by the above percentages, is an emotional one. Only 9 percent of women who were not interfered with indicated migraine headaches, but three times as many women in each of the other two groups suffered such headaches.

Do we need to understand all the biological and physiological ramifications of migraine headaches? In many cases, apparently not. If the real cause of the distress is found in childhood trauma, then the Lord and the victim working together can bring about healing. If the stress resulting from the trauma is cleansed and healed, will not the recurrence of migraine headaches then cease? The reasonable answer must be a strong affirmative, for the Lord came to heal all manner of disease.

3. Marital Sexual Disinterest

Among the women responding to the survey, further studies were done to determine the effect of childhood sexual trauma on marital relationships. Not surprisingly, the results were similar to the other two strong symptoms already described.

No sexual interference	14.7%
Yes—Acknowledged	35.8%
Yes—Suppressed	26.6%

These figures were for all women in the sample groups, including married, never married, divorced and remarried.

A disruption in God's plan for the healthy development of a child's body and emotions will have long-term damaging effects on the grown woman's opportunity to have a healthy marital relationship.

4. Affairs During Marriage

The findings of this symptom in the sample groups surprised us. First, we were surprised at the similarity of percentages between the groups. We would have expected a higher percentage among those victimized than among those who were not, but there was virtually no difference. Second, we were surprised at the percentage of Christian women who acknowledged having affairs during marriage. If we compared the number of yes responses to the total number of *married* women taking the survey (this sample included never-married women as well), the percentages would have been even higher. We must also consider the possibility that, while filling out the survey, a woman seated close to someone else may be reluctant to answer and would skip over "Affairs During Marriage."

No sexual interference	12.5%
Yes—Acknowledged	12.0%

Yes—Suppressed 8.5%

The information that has been presented here is not intended to shock or to startle, but to alert the body of believers to the depths of the problems that do exist. Individuals who are emotionally bound by childhood trauma become an ineffective force in service and ministry. Their available energy is so consumed and drained with their struggles, trying to break the bands of their bondage, that they are unable, unwilling or unaware they can function as God intended.

It is from the heart of our love for the Lord Jesus Christ, rather than from duty or responsibility, that we who are healthy or have been healed from similar afflictions desire to comfort those who are presently suffering with the comfort with which we ourselves have been comforted.

General Conclusions

Gradually, the church is becoming aware that there is a monster in its midst. For years the presence and the practice of childhood sexual abuse was thought to be a rare aberration that touched few of us in our congregations personally. However, the number of Christian books recently written, purchased and absorbed by eager readers who are hungry for hope, help and healing, is a clear indication that Christians are becoming aware of the depth and the prevalence of the problem.

The findings of our survey have been corroborated by numerous credentialed Christian counselors. Some have even told us that the figures may be too conservative.

According to our survey, it is possible that three-fourths of all women in the church today have been victims of some form of childhood sexual interference. This is having devastating manifestations in their adult lives, keeping them bound, preventing them from fully knowing, loving and serving their Lord. Of these women who apparently have suffered interference, only one-third are aware of it and the remaining two-thirds have no knowledge of it at all.

Picture a meeting of one hundred women in your church today. Twenty-five of those women, sitting on the left side, acknowledge and are aware of some form of victimization in their childhood and are today living the consequences of those childhood experiences. Another twenty-five, sitting on the right side, have been fortunate to have escaped childhood trauma and are living adult lives reasonably free of distress and turmoil. The other group of fifty, sitting in the center, did experience childhood sexual trauma but have no conscious awareness of it. They are probably coming to church on Sunday morning with their "happy faces" carefully glued on, but are unable, for some unknown reason, to live during the week the abundant and fulfilled life that Christ promised to them. They have no idea why, or what may be the source of their pains and problems.

Figures for men are only slightly less dramatic. While six out of ten men show evidence of having experienced childhood interference, only one in ten is aware of it. The remaining five, or 50 percent of all men, have no such knowledge.

These are people who are deeply hurting inside. They may not be dysfunctional, so we do not recognize the depth of their pain. Their pleasant Sunday morning smiles belie the turmoil and stress within themselves or in their home. The church wonders why we cannot get our people involved, active and serving. Why are they not growing spiritually? Why is the church not growing numerically? People who are so consumed with the daily strain of keeping their lives together have no energy left for effectively serving the Savior.

Robert Schuller has often said, "If you want to build your church, find your community's need and fill it." Several months ago, Florence and I were speaking at a denominational pastors' and wives' retreat. During one presentation, I asked the assembled group, "How many of you, in your church, have any kind of ministry, meetings or support groups for alcoholics?" I looked around the room, waiting for hands to be raised. Not one!

I asked again, "How many of you have any kind of ministry for people who are divorced?" Not one hand went up!

"How many of you have any ministry, counseling or support groups for victims of sexual abuse?" This time I was prepared for the response. It was the same . . . not one.

I am convinced that childhood sexual interference is our nation's number-one scourge today. And if it is the nation's, then it is the church's number-one problem as well. Alcoholism, divorce and drugs are generally derivatives of this root problem. It has been with us for centuries upon centuries. Avoiding it, not facing it or denying it does not make it disappear.

People are hurting. Pastors generally have no understanding of the issue or how to deal with it, and they send the seeker elsewhere—often to secular counseling or therapy which, in too many situations, may be best described as horrible. Frequently the "counselor" is a wounded healer himself.[1] Even few Christian counselors have a clear sense of the steps a victim must take on the journey to healing.

If the church does not provide the resources for healing of emotional bondage, we are telling the victim to go elsewhere. In the ninth chapter of Mark, when the disciples could not cast the spirit out of the boy, Jesus said, "Bring him unto me" (verse 19). Jesus stated that He came to heal the brokenhearted, to set the captives free, to release those in bondage. Is it not to His church, then, that the brokenhearted and bound should come today? Healing is spiritual; it is not psychological. Jesus is the only One who can heal. Guiding and counseling the one who needs healing requires understanding, compassion, knowledge, experience and ultimately wisdom. Should not the victim expect to find such comfort and spiritual counsel in his church?

More and more churches today are recognizing the need and providing counseling services and support groups. But we are only beginning to scratch the surface. The church that will aggressively face the issue, provide the resources, personnel and facilities, and communicate the availability, will find people coming from everywhere. We are in an era when it is becoming less of a stigma for a person to say, "I was molested as a child and I need help today."

Let us, the church, be sure we are providing the help that is needed.

9

TAKING THE SURVEY

If the findings of the "Survey of Emotions and Experience" are valid, then an additional 50 percent of all men (above the acknowledged 10 percent) and 50 percent of all women (above the acknowledged 25 percent) have some form of childhood interference of which they are completely unaware.

There are many different *kinds*, *forms* and *types* of childhood sexual interference. We use the term "interference" rather than "sexual abuse" because the latter tends to create a mental picture in people's minds of a child being hideously attacked and ravaged. That vile and horrible form of abuse does occur, but there are many other ways in which God's design can be distorted and the child's life devastated. The long-term effects of some of the other forms can be no less destructive to the child's adult health and happiness. Different forms of interference affect different people in radically different ways. Even two children in the same family suffering the same treatment may have markedly different adult manifestations. There are no hard and fast rules of understanding, interpretation or expectation.

Kinds, Types and Forms of Interference

There are three *kinds* of interference: emotional, visual and physical.

Emotional interference occurs when a child is made to feel, by whatever method or means, that anything sexual is bad, nasty or evil. A mother who continually foments the notion that sex is disgusting will plant in her daughter unhealthy and erroneous seeds of thought which may grow into a sickly sexual attitude in adulthood.

Visual interference occurs when a child's view of sexuality is distorted by seeing sexual activities of an inappropriate or unhealthy nature. For example: continued exposure to explicit videos or magazines, or observance of unnatural acts in the home.

Physical interference refers to any sexual contact between a child and another person. Though the perpetrator is usually older or an adult, even inappropriate contact between children can activate the recipient child's dormant sexuality.

Types of Sexual Interference

In addition to the three *kinds* of interference, it is important to recognize the three basic *types* of sexual interference: seductive, subjugation, and Satanic or ritualistic.

Seductive is a non-threatening type of abuse which combines loving treatment with sexual molestation. The child is told he or she is very special right from the beginning and may receive gifts, favors and extra treats after each sexual encounter. The child who has no frame of reference for parental love assumes this must be the way daddies or mommies behave and yet inside there is a feeling of guilt that belies the words of affection.

Subjugation is when the violator takes pleasure in exerting power over the victim. The idea of sexual contact is not only for gratification but also for control over another person who is smaller, weaker and unable to fight back. The molester usually has an extremely low self-image and has often been abused as a child himself. The perpetrator is often a brother who wants to conquer little sister, or a stepfather who feels he is owed something in return for supplying a home for the child.

Satanic interference involves highly abusive sexual acts; these may even include brutal torture—a violence so repugnant that healthy minds cannot even comprehend the possibility. Details of such trauma are being increasingly revealed through Holy Spirit-guided memory retrieval, including satanic circumcision on little girls.

Forms of Sexual Interference

In addition to three basic kinds of interference and three basic types of abuse, we also have four *forms* of sexual interference:

1. *Suppression*—all normal sexual inquiry, expression and feelings are reprimanded. This is most often verbal or visual in nature.

2. *Exploitation*—inappropriate exposure of victim's or perpetrator's body for sexually satisfying purposes.

3. *Molestation*—sexually oriented touching or fondling of victim by perpetrator, by victim of perpetrator or both.

4. *Penetration*—oral, vaginal or anal insertion by penile, digital or gadgetal means.

Childhood sexual interference (the disruption or distortion of God's design for the normal and healthy development of the child's body and emotions) may include any one or a combination of these kinds, types and forms described above. Any one of these alone can be emotionally devastating to the adult, and some trauma can be the cause of severe physical manifestations and undiagnosable pains. It is important to understand, when searching for truth or praying for healing, that acknowledging the symptom may reveal the source, and we must be willing to accept that possibility. An individual who reacts with hostility or sharp denial to even the possibility of any childhood interference is generally unconsciously suppressing a trauma that he may be unwilling to concede. Such sharp reaction is like steam escaping from a pressure cooker. Simply saying there is no steam in the cooker because you can't see it does not eliminate the fact of its existence.

It is necessary to dig out the sin, if there was sin committed against you; it is necessary to "take out the trash." You have a right to know the truth. Are you ready to take the survey yourself? Are you ready to stand before your Lord and accept His offer, "Ye shall know the truth"?

SURVEY OF EMOTIONS AND EXPERIENCE

Please check each box that applies or has ever applied to you. Leave blank any that do not apply or you are not sure of. (This survey is a slightly modified version of the one we used in the research project.)

Abortion ❑
Affairs during marriage ❑
•• Alcoholic parent ❑
•• Anorexia or bulimia ❑
•• Brother or sister molested as a child ❑
• Childhood "bad houses or rooms" ❑
Childhood depression ❑
•• Downcast looks as a child ❑
• Early childhood anger ❑
• Early childhood masturbation ❑
Emotionally abused as a child ❑
Emotions suppressed in childhood ❑
•• Fear of being alone ❑
•• Fear of losing weight ❑
• Feel unworthy of God's love ❑
• Feeling "dirty" ❑
• Fits of rage ❑
Guilt feelings ❑
• Hate men ❑
Hide real feelings ❑
• Lack of resistance to sexual attack ❑
•• Lack of trust ❑
Low self-worth ❑
Marital sexual disinterest ❑
• Memory gaps in childhood ❑

- •• Migraine headaches ❑
- Nudity forbidden in childhood family ❑
- • Obsessive fear of rape ❑
- • Panic attacks ❑
- Physically abused as child ❑
- •• PMS ❑
- Poor teenage opposite sex relations ❑
- • Recurring bad dreams ❑
- Rejection feelings ❑
- • Same sex attraction ❑
- Sexually abused or molested as a child ❑
- • Sexual compulsions ❑
- Suicidal feelings ❑
- Teenage promiscuity ❑
- • Temptation to touch children sexually ❑
- Tendency to overreact ❑
- • Uncomfortable with nudity in marriage ❑
- •• Uncontrollable anger ❑
- • Uncontrollable crying ❑
- •• Undiagnosed pains and aches ❑

Add up the total number of boxes you have checked and put the number in the space labeled *Total.* Then go back and circle every symptom you have checked that has one dot in front of it. Now write in your total of one-dot symptoms.

Total_______ **Total with one dot_______**

Some of us have had very hurtful experiences as children. Some of us have suffered vicious acts to our bodies or emotions. Some of us had our spirits broken by adults who didn't realize what they were doing. Sometimes they did know; sometimes we were knowingly hurt.

Some of us remember quite well what happened but for others the memories are hazy. For some of you, there are no memories, yet deep inside you may be feeling, "Some of this applies to me." You may find yourself "feeling things," sobbing or crying uncontrollably. Your body may shake or quiver. Your emotions may be remembering what your mind has forgotten.

If this is happening to you, stop reading for the time being. Give yourself a rest and a change. Before continuing, follow these recommendations:

Take out a sheet of paper and write a prayer to your Father in heaven. Tell Him how you are feeling. Tell Him about the emotions that are coming up. Tell Him you are scared. Ask Him to help you. Ask Him to comfort you, to give you strength. He understands how you feel. He has suffered even as you have. He has suffered more, for He accepted the excruciating death of crucifixion that you might be set free and restored completely:

> I have come that you might have life, and that you might have it abundantly (John 10:10).
>
> I have come to heal the brokenhearted, to set the captive free, the release of those who are in bondage (Isaiah 61:1; Luke 4:18, paraphrased).
>
> He was made like you and me in all things, since He Himself was tempted, tested, in that which He suffered, He is able to come to the aid of those who suffered (Hebrews 2:17,18, paraphrased).
>
> We do not have a high priest who cannot sympathize with our weaknesses, but one who has been tempted in all things. . . . Let us, therefore draw near with confidence to the throne of grace, that we may receive mercy and may find grace to help in time of need (Hebrews 4:15,16, NASB).

Further, He promises this to you:

> No temptation [trial or testing] has overtaken you but such as is common to man; and God is faithful, who will not allow you to be tempted beyond what you are able; but with the temptation will provide the way of escape also, that you may be able to endure it (1 Corinthians 10:13, NASB).

In the prayer you are writing, claim these promises for yourself. Tell Him you want to be free of the hurt that is inside you. Ask Him to help you. He will if you ask. Continue writing until you feel His peace and your emotions are calm and quiet. Be sure to praise Him and thank Him for listening to you and for always being there when you need Him. (Even if you don't *feel* it, He is there for you!)

Do not proceed further, if there are emotions welling up uncontrollably, without seeking the help of a trusted, non-judgmental family member or friend who will support you, encourage you, pray with you and comfort you. Unless your support person is a spouse, adult child, or pastor, he or she must be the same sex as you.

We also strongly recommend that you seek the help of a *qualified Christian* therapist, counselor or pastor who is trained and experienced in the gentle recollection and resolution of childhood trauma.

Understanding Your Survey Results

Everything listed on the survey, except one, is a possible symptom of childhood sexual interference. "Sexually abused or molested as a child" is not a symptom; it is a known fact. If you checked that item, you already know that there was, in fact, some form of interference in your childhood. You may have clear memories or they may be dim, but you do know something happened.

Look back at your survey. How many one-dot symptoms did you check? Remember that one-dot symptoms are clear symptoms. We believe that the presence of only one of these is a clear indication of some inappropriate sexual activity in your childhood, even if you have absolutely no knowledge of it. Refer to the last chapter in which I explained the one-dot symptoms. The more one-dot symptoms you check further confirms what you may be discovering about yourself.

Those symptoms checked that have two dots in front of them are "strong" symptoms. One of them alone on your list is not enough to indicate childhood interference because its presence can sometimes be traced to other sources. However, a significant number of two-dot symptoms, even without any of the one-dot symptoms, is cause enough for you to continue your search for truth and for cleansing and healing of the troubling emotions you may be facing. Even if there is no sexual interference, the steps of healing which will be outlined apply to you, for your two-dot symptoms may be the result of emotional deprivation or rejection.

The symptoms with no dots are considered to be only "possible" symptoms. They may, in conjunction with the other symptoms, give a valid picture of experiences and emotions you may never have thought about.

Emotions and Anger

If you have reacted emotionally to your list or to the explanation of the symptoms, that may be an important signal for you. Our emotions remember what our mind has forgotten. Grant yourself the privilege and the right to know. Jesus said, "Ye *shall* know the truth" (John 8:32). He granted you the right to know. Begin by praying and asking God to reveal to you anything you need to see from your childhood. He has both the power and the knowledge to do that. After all, He knows what happened to you, even if you don't. He was there all the time.

If you have reacted with anger to the explanation of what you have checked on your own list, you may think, *That's impossible! That's ridiculous! This is too simple. How can they say all those things are connected with sexual abuse? How can they make such conclusions in just a few minutes with this short survey? How do I know this is accurate?* If some of these reactions of anger fit your feelings, this could also be an important signal. The person with no "trash in his past" does not react in anger.

You might ask yourself, "Where did my anger come from if it's not from interference?" Did God put it into you when you were born? Or did someone else put it into you afterward?

Anger at sin and evil is a healthy, God-given emotion. But to react in anger to some words you read in a book? Is that God-given? Or is it a reaction, a stirring up of some deeply suppressed feelings? In counseling many hundreds of hurting adults, I have *never* met a person who reacted angrily to the possibility of sexual interference who was not a victim to such interference in his childhood, even though they themselves had no knowledge of it at the time.

Denial

If the survey revealed the possibility of sexual interference in your childhood, did you react with: "That's impossible"; or "I had a perfect childhood"; or "I come from a good Christian home"; or "I checked off some of those one-dot things, but I *know* I was not sexually abused"? Once again, your *reaction* could be significant. It is possible that you are in *denial,* an unwillingness to face or even consider the truth.

Your denial does not mean that it could not have happened. Because you do not remember any such thing does not mean it isn't there. Do you remember every moment of your childhood? We only remember what we remember. All of us have experiences and events, things that were said to us or things done to us that have slipped away into the murky past, never to be heard from again. How, then, can one be so sure?

Please understand: We do not want you to search and agonize over something that isn't there. We have no interest in a "witch hunt" that arbitrarily pegs sexual interference as the cause of adult problems. But we do feel obligated to alert today's adults to the common denominators we have discovered in this crucial area.

Allow yourself to consider the possibility. Are there some adult issues in your life with which you are not happy, with which you don't think God is happy? If you don't feel God is blessing you right now with blessing upon blessing; if there is anger, depression, compulsions or feelings of rejection over which you have not been able to get victory; if you have prayed and prayed, and studied and studied, and still there is no improvement, perhaps now is the time to ask yourself, "Could it be possible? Is there something in my childhood that is still affecting me today? Is there some reason I have made so many poor choices in my life? Is there some reason I feel like a failure? Is there some unknown reason my marriage is unsatisfying?"

Are you willing to pray, "Open thou mine eyes, that I may behold wondrous things out of the law"? (Psalm 119:18)

He will open your eyes if you ask. But you must ask, and you must desire to know the truth. God is unlikely to force on you that which you refuse to see.

An Important Question

Having evaluated your survey and listened to your emotional reactions, you may gain some understanding of what might have happened to you. Even though you may not have clear knowledge, you may now be aware that there is something worth looking into. A relatively simple step can shed significant light on what you may be seeking.

As you look over your own survey, if you find you have checked *none* of the one-dot symptoms, only a few of those with two dots or only a small number in total (five to twelve with no one-dot symptoms), there is very little likelihood you suffered any sexual interference in your childhood. You may want to skip over the rest of this section and proceed to the Promise of Healing. There may be some other issues in your life for which you would like cleansing and healing from the Lord. The most common is rejection.

If you cannot answer yes with certainty to the following question, you may be feeling the pains of emotional deprivation.

> As a child, did you *feel* loved, especially by your parents or guardians?

Notice the question was not "Did your parents love you? but "Did you *feel* loved?" There is a big difference. Most parents do love their children to the best of their ability. But if they, themselves, did not feel loved as children, they may have a weak frame of reference to know how to give their own children the feeling of being loved. If, in addition, your parents had to deal with other deep issues in their lives which resulted in anger, depression, financial problems, single parenting or alcoholism (to name a few), they may not have had the time or the ability to give you the healthy nurturing you needed and desired as a child.

Again, the question:

> Did you feel loved as a child? Yes_____ No_____

If you answered "No" to feeling loved, or if you were not sure, you probably do have some feelings that need healing. You may be ensnared in the trap of rejection. If that is the case, the steps of healing apply as effectively to you and will provide the same benefit if you follow them.

Invariably, victims of sexual interference are also victims of rejection. If the victimization took place in the home, all the dynamics of the child's, and later the adult's, emotions will cause feelings of having been neglected, unprotected or rejected, of not being good enough or acceptable. The child may have been put on a performance-based approval and value system. This means, then, that the adult victim must deal with these two major issues.

In the literally hundreds of men and women whom I have met and guided, I can remember only one victim of molestation who was not also a victim of rejection. This was a woman whose home environment was loving, secure and supportive. She was molested by a male neighbor, a perpetrator from outside the home. When the child did report the offense to her parents, she felt supported and cared for. Rejection was not an issue, but she was still dealing with the effects of the molestation.

If you answered yes to the question, "Did you feel loved as a child?" and from survey results you are confident there is no interference in your childhood, give heartfelt thanks to the Lord. You are one of a very small group relatively free of these childhood scars. You will probably want to skip over the next few chapters and proceed to the Promise of Healing. You may gain some insights that will give you a relationship with your Lord you never before dreamed could exist.

10

TOUGH QUESTIONS, IMPORTANT ANSWERS

This chapter contains questions and explanations of an explicit nature and should be avoided by anyone who might be offended by such material.

The questions and discussions are not intended to be shocking or distasteful. They relate specifically to real experiences that countless Christians have faced at some time in their life. The intent is to enable the reader to discover the truth as quickly as possible, to uncover any sin that might have been committed against him, while keeping the pain to a minimum so that the journey of restoration may be more readily begun. For scriptural authority, once again refer to Joshua 7 and see how quickly God moved to uncover and destroy the sin that was buried in Achan's tent. If you feel you might be offended, please skip this chapter.

The answers you give to the following personal questions will help you understand and be prepared for what the Lord may reveal to you if you desire Holy Spirit-guided memory retrieval. You will be answering the questions only for your own benefit or to assist your counselor in guiding you. To protect your privacy you may want to write your responses on a separate piece of paper.

Read the questions carefully and answer them as accurately as you can after giving careful thought to your feelings. You are not only looking for facts, but for *emotional reactions* as well. The way you react to the questions is important and may be a key to what might have happened. The Holy Spirit can reveal to you the who, the when and the where.

1. As a child, do you remember playing with yourself sexually? Yes______No______

a. If you answered Yes, think back to your childhood. What do you think was the earliest age at which you did? (To help you estimate, think of where you were, what room, house or apartment, what grade in school.) Age _______

b. Was it a once-or-twice experience, or something you did often? Often ______ Not Often______

c. Would you describe your feelings as compulsive? Yes ______No ______

d. As an adult, would you say those childhood feelings were sexual? Yes______ No______

2. (Women only) Can you remember the very *first* time you experienced sexual intercourse? Yes______No______

a. Do you remember who you were with? Yes ______ No ______

b. Do you remember where you were? Yes ______ No______

c. Was there sharp pain?______ Blood?______

d. If you don't remember, think again about where you were and the circumstances. Did you find spotting later? _______

3. (This question is applicable only to women and men who are or have been married). How do you feel about oral sex? (Note: The issue is not whether you think it is right or wrong, but how you *feel* emotionally about it.) Please check off all words that express your feelings:

1. ❑ Crave it	5. ❑ Hate it	9. ❑ Okay
2. ❑ Disgusting	6. ❑ Like it	10. ❑ Revolting
3. ❑ Exciting	7. ❑ Nauseating	11. ❑ Satisfying
4. ❑ Gross	8. ❑ No problem	12. ❑ Yuk!

a. In answering the above question were you primarily thinking of giving_____, or receiving_____?

4. Have you at any time in your life had a sexual experience with a person of the same sex?

Child (5 to 9)	Yes_____	No_____
Youth (10 to 12)	Yes_____	No_____
Teen	Yes_____	No_____
Adult	Yes_____	No_____

a. If you answered yes on any line above, think back to the event(s). Whose idea was it? Yours_____ Other person_____

b. If you were the follower, were you willing_____, passive (uncaring)_____ or resistant_____?

5. If you are aware of some interference or molestation in your childhood, what was the earliest age at which you think it happened? _____

a. In thinking back to that first time, do you think you were willing_____, just let it happen_____ or resistant_____?

6. Is there any adult figure in your childhood whom you remember hating, being afraid of or hiding from? If so, write the name or description below, then explain why you feel the way you do.

1. ____

____

2.____

____

3.____

____

What Your Answers May Reveal

1. Playing With Yourself as a Child

It is normal for a child to explore and become familiar with his or her body. It is healthy for a child to like and be happy with his body. A parent would be well advised never to scold or scream at a child who is simply becoming acquainted with himself.

On the other hand, it should not be considered healthy or normal for a child to play with himself in such a way as to get sexually satisfying feelings. When God created our bodies, He built in a normal, healthy sexuality. That capacity, however, was not designed to be developed or activated until puberty. When a child plays with himself prior to puberty, in such a manner as to make him or herself "feel good," that is a sign that his sexuality has been prematurely activated.

Among specialists there is general agreement that a young child cannot activate his or her own sexuality; there must be an outside stimulus. A child of three, four or five years of age, for example, has no knowledge or understanding of sexuality. The sexual parts of his or her body have no more "feeling" than an ear lobe.

Therefore, when a child is playing with himself sexually at any age prior to puberty, there must have been something or someone which caused him to be activated. That stimulus is invariably some form of molestation. If the child's activity becomes frequent and compulsive, it may well indicate a more frequent or severe molestation.

If you answered yes to question number one, there is a very strong possibility that someone, somewhere, at some time, fondled or touched you inappropriately. That you cannot remember any such thing is no assurance that it never happened.

The age at which you began touching yourself is significant for two reasons. First, it may give you a clue as to the time and place, or who might have been in your life at that time, to help you identify who the possible perpetrator might be. Second, it will help you determine whether to look earlier into your life. If you estimate you were eight to ten, you may want to focus back to an earlier age. We have found that most interference takes place between the ages of three to five, especially for little girls. Children between the ages of eight and ten have a more fully developed sense of right and wrong in addition to being in a better position to protect themselves, refuse or run.

Little children of three to five have little opportunity or strength to protect themselves. A fundamental principle they are learning at this age is obedience. They have little capacity to sort out in their minds when obedience is appropriate and when it is not. The emotional dynamics going on in a little child's mind are complex and there are no simplistic or dogmatic certainties.

Your yes answer to question number one should be taken as an indication that some form of physical interference may have been committed against your body as a child. This is the first step in coming to the point of facing the reality and finding the source of your present emotional struggles.

2. Your First Sexual Experience

The entire purpose of this question, which is applicable to women only, is to help you determine whether your virginity was intact at your first sexual encounter, whenever it might have been. Who you were with and where you were is only significant in helping you ascertain an accurate conclusion.

If a woman, after searching her memories and rethinking the situation and circumstances, cannot remember pain or blood in connection with her first sexual experience, she is gently shown that there is a possibility that her hymen was ruptured at some earlier time in her life, perhaps even in childhood. This prepares her for what the Holy Spirit may later reveal to her through flashbacks or memory retrieval.

The question is frequently asked, "Couldn't this happen from athletics or accidents?" The answer is always, yes it could, but its incidence is rare. The far more common explanation is some form of childhood vaginal penetration. When the mind is ready to accept this as a possibility, the way is prepared for the Holy Spirit to reveal the truth.

3. Feelings in the Marital Relationship

These questions may be the most significant in your search for truth. The explanation of your answers may surprise you more than any of the others. Emotional reactions may surface that you didn't know were there. The explanation may cause strong feelings of hostility or denial. It may also help you get quickly to the root of some of the issues you are facing. It may explain some of the feelings or fears in your life today.

Sandy, whose story you will be reading shortly, said of her psychiatrist, to whom she paid regular visits for five years, "He only cut down the weeds. He never dug out the root and so the weeds kept growing back." Digging out the root of the weeds is not easy, nor is it always pleasant. Sometimes, when we dig deeply, rot and stench that has been festering for years is uncovered. A woman with whom I met in Australia told me she had been pulling away "cobwebs" in her life for years, but she had never found the "spider." He kept making new webs. The day I talked with her, the Holy Spirit uncovered the spider through memory retrieval. Once brought to the light, the spider was killed, never more to spin cobwebs of bondage.

During the time of my own intensive counseling, the Lord gave me a phrase which I have not forgotten. I know it was from Him because it has proven to be true over and over: "Awareness is the first step to freedom." The authority of Scripture continually confirms it.

In question number three, if you checked lines three, six, eight, nine or eleven, you have indicated emotional responses which hint at no apparent childhood violation in this area. The answers more frequently given by victims are: *disgusting, gross, hate it, nauseating, revolting* or *yuk!* These answers are usually accompanied with passion and intensity. Disgusting! Gross! Revolting! This type of impassioned, highly negative response can be taken as powerful evidence of childhood oral violation. This is one of the most common forms of violations on little boys and girls, perpetrated by both men and women to satisfy their compulsive cravings.

How anyone could commit such a violation I cannot answer. I presume that the victimizer considers it relatively harmless, not having any idea of the extreme devastation wrought on the child. I presume that they never consider it rape, thinking it is not physically damaging or vicious. And it leaves no tell-tale traces to come back and haunt the perpetrator. Oral abuse is often seductive in nature, and the child, usually a little girl, is told she is "good" if she allows repeated violations. Threats may be added to protect the adult and insure secrecy. If the child does complain, usually the adult whom she tells finds the child's claims so incredulous that he or she tends to believe the powerful protestations of innocence of the perpetrator.

One woman at a recent conference told Florence that when she told her mother and father what Grandpa was doing to her, they promptly drove over to Grandpa's house to give the child the opportunity to confront him in their presence. She felt more like the accused rather than the accuser. The grandfather vehemently denied the child's allegations, took her father into another room and told him his daughter was absolutely lying. The mother and father believed the grandfather, and on the way home the child was severely scolded for making up such bad lies. The child's protection had been stripped away, and in the next couple of years the parents would occasionally drop the child off at her grandparents to be babysat. As you may have suspected, the oral abuse violations continued. There was no evidence, no telltale traces. The child was powerless.

A very high percentage of women who have asked the Holy Spirit to reveal the truth and to retrieve their memories have found they were victims of oral abuse. Many have actually re-experienced the horrifying characteristics of choking and gagging. This form of abuse is especially frequent when the child is three to five years old.

However, it is not only men who are guilty of this form of abuse. Many men, under the guidance of the Holy Spirit, found themselves as children being coerced or seduced into satisfying the lustful cravings of a mother, a grandmother, a babysitter or a female neighbor. I met with a man not long ago who had no knowledge of any interference in his childhood, but readily admitted he had many of the adult symptoms, including sexual compulsions. As the Holy Spirit guided him back into his childhood experiences, he found himself visiting a neighbor who allowed him to come to her house to watch television. Since he didn't have one in his home this was a special treat. She also served him milk and cookies. But there was a price he had to pay for these treats. He was called into her room where he had to orally satisfy her physical cravings.

A young pastor who asked to see Florence after a recent conference told her of his childhood experience with the lady down the street who every week or so had the little boys in the neighborhood come in for ice cream and cake. All the parents thought, "Isn't she sweet!"

What the parents never knew, he continued, was that "after ice cream, we all had to take our pants off and she played tag with us, tagging us in special places. After we finished playing tag, we would play spin the bottle, and whoever 'won' would get to go in her bedroom for a while, with the door closed." The boys were always told, "Keep our little party a secret, or you might not be allowed to come again."

The young pastor asked to see Florence because he was struggling in his pastorate as well as in his marriage. He had never considered that these little parties were the root cause of many of his personal, marital and spiritual stresses. In addition, he had many of the classic symptoms of a victim, initially stemming from the "nice" lady down the street.

Part a of question number three, regarding giving or receiving, may help you further define your feelings. As you think about your responses, if there was oral violation in your childhood, you may have a clearer insight whether the victimizer was male or female.

Response number one to question number three, "Crave it," has not yet been discussed. This response is less frequently given. The usual source of this feeling is that the child was orally violated in a seductive manner—rarely with fear or coercion, and usually with approval, appreciation and possibly with gifts. "Crave it" generally results from repeated violations over an extended time in which the abuse became not only the normal and accepted way of life, but possibly an experience eagerly anticipated by the child because of the resulting affirmation. The child (and now the adult) may have become addicted. Even though the experience itself, from the child's perspective, might have seemed totally positive, it is often completely blocked out of conscious adult memory. Although the childhood experience did not seem to be devastatingly traumatic, the adult will more than likely have manifestations which are as equally severe as if the violation had been traumatic.

Your responses to this question may be taken as a clear indication of your childhood experiences. If you are already in counseling, we encourage you to share your conclusions with your counselor, particularly if these questions have not yet been raised. If you are contemplating counseling, promptly sharing this with your counselor may reduce the time required to get to the root of your problems. Many counselors are not in the habit of searching for the sources as quickly as has been presented to you here. Many other counselors, unfortunately, deal only with the symptoms, trying to help you change your behavior without curing the root that the fruit may become good, clearing cobwebs without killing the spider.

4. Same-Sex Relationships

Your answers to these questions, if you are now suspecting or acknowledging the possibility of interference in your childhood, will further help you focus on who the violator might be and when the first incident may have occurred.

Our findings indicate that a person who now has, or has had, same-sex attraction and experiences, or in some cases even only fantasies, must have been sexually interfered with at some time. Question four will help you focus on when these things may have happened. Questions a and b will help determine if it was, in fact, the first time. If you were the initiator, as a child especially (but even as a youth or teen), that must be considered strong evidence that there was earlier interference. Otherwise, why would you have thought or felt like doing the things you did?

On the other hand, any resistance on your part reveals the extent of your defense mechanisms. You may have acquiesced because the person was someone whose love, attention or respect you didn't want to lose. This would be especially important to you if you did not feel loved at home. Your feelings of rejection caused you to be vulnerable. Feelings of passivity toward the act might indicate a low self-esteem. You felt your body was not worth anything, so what did it matter?

It is important to think about your feelings and emotions. When probing for possible answers, we always want to stress how the healthy non-interfered child would react or respond. If your feelings and emotions were different, ask yourself why. Why did you give in? Why did you not say no? Why did you not run away? Why did you think it would be fun to do? Why did you have sexual feelings before your sexuality was developed? Your own answers to these questions will help you sharpen your focus as you ask the Holy Spirit to guide you into truth. Some suggestions on how to do this will be offered later.

5. Earliest Molestation

This question is primarily for persons who are aware of some interference, but suspect there may be more. The purposes and insights are similar to that which has been presented in number four above.

The preceding five questions are designed to help you understand your own findings on your survey form and, if there is any possibility of interference in God's design for your healthy development, to give more specific insight to what you might have endured as a child.

The answers to the survey are based on *facts* and your awareness of them. The answers to the questions in this chapter are based more on *feelings* and what those feelings might reveal about unknown facts. Your own willingness to be objective and to allow yourself the right to know may have affected what you have learned about yourself. The survey, originally designed for research purposes and now used in slightly modified form in counseling situations, has been found to be remarkably accurate in determining the possibility of childhood trauma. The questions that were presented to you for your own search for truth were developed over a period of time and, when used by a skilled and experienced counselor in evaluating the answers, have been found to be relatively unerring.

6. Fearful Figures

At this point, through your responses and your reactions, you may have a fairly clear concept of what might have happened to you. To help you see who might have been responsible for today's feelings and pains, this question focuses on some adult figures from your childhood who give you bad or negative feelings.

Once again, by asking yourself "Why?," you are seeking out the reason you might have had such feelings. You will find that the more you pursue these issues in your life, the more likely you will be to have dreams, flashbacks and feelings that all seem to focus on or around this subject. That is both normal and healthy in digging up the root of the sin that may have been committed against you. As you think of those people you hated, were afraid of or hid from in your childhood, you may find they connect with some of the other emotions you are feeling. You may find that they were present in your life during the time of some of the experiences you may have remembered. There is a chance that one or more of the persons you have named may be connected with a perpetration.

In searching for truth you must be willing to look at anyone and everyone as a possibility, until the Holy Spirit clearly reveals the identity of the one you are looking for. You must be ready and willing to know the truth, without restriction or reservation. We often hear, "I could handle it being anybody but my grandfather. He was my only support system." Or "I hate my father, but I couldn't handle it being him." Or "It couldn't possibly be my mother, even though she was an alcoholic."

Even though the victim intellectually wants to know, emotionally he or she may be blocking the truth. As you pray to the Holy Spirit to guide you into all truth, to bring all things to your remembrance, He will probably never require you to see what you don't want to see. You must be willing, without reservation, to know the truth, no matter upon whose shoulders the responsibility may fall. If you don't really have the unreserved desire to know, begin praying now—ask the Lord to give you that desire.

> What woman, having ten silver coins [or years] if she loses one coin [or year] does not *light a lamp* and *sweep the house* and *search diligently* until she finds it? (Luke 15:8, NASB).

11

THE MIRROR OF YOUR SOUL

What do the eyes reveal? "The lamp of the body is the eye, if therefore your eye is clear [healthy] your whole body will be full of light. But if your eye is bad your whole body will be full of darkness" (Matthew 6:22, NASB).

Is it not true that if your body is full of light, your eyes will express that light? And that if your body, your heart, your emotions are full of darkness, your eyes will express that darkness and pain, that fear, anger or sadness?

Gather all the childhood pictures you can and arrange them in sequential order, beginning with the earliest. Look particularly for pictures that reveal your eyes. Don't use any pictures that are dark, shaded or unclear, where the eyes cannot be seen.

Usually the earliest picture will be of a happy child. His eyes will look clear and bright. As you look at the pictures and watch the child grow older, do you still see a bright, clear look in the eyes? Or has there been a change at some point? The camera captures and records forever the feelings of the child at that given moment.

What do you see in your childhood pictures? Any changes, especially when they seem to continue into subsequent years, may pinpoint almost the very time when a child suffered some experience that so altered his inner nature that it was reflected in his eyes.

While you are looking at your collection of pictures, notice also the location, setting, other people in the picture, plants, trees, even family cars. If there are years that have disappeared from your memory, a single item in one picture may be a key to gradually opening up the memory of where you were, what you did, who was with you. Faces of long-forgotten relatives may suddenly be looking at you—perhaps someone you didn't like or were afraid of.

Learn to "read" the pictures. See what they may reveal to you. Study the eyes—they are the lamp of the body.

Here are some pictures for you to read. Look at each one carefully and then on the lines below write your description of the child or the young man. How do you think he is feeling? Write down anything that comes to your mind. *Important:* Do not skip over this section. Carefully study these four pictures.

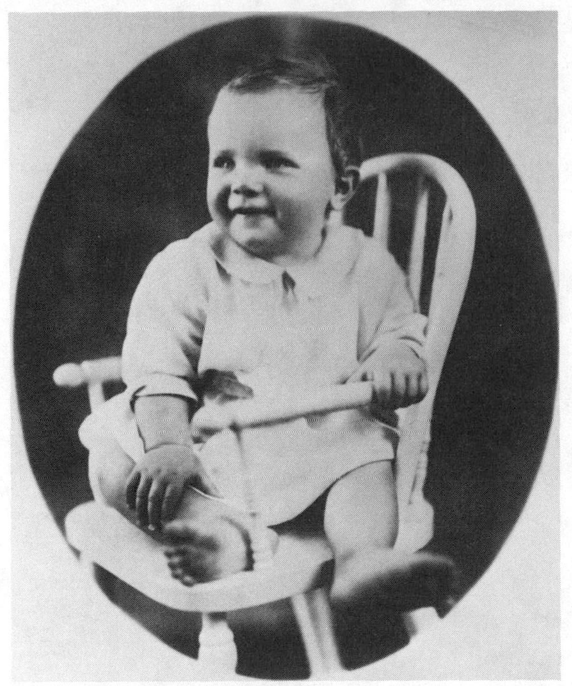

How does this baby boy feel? ______________________

____

____

____

How do you feel about him? ______________________

____

____

____

How old do you think he is? ________________

How does this little boy feel?______________________

____

____

____

What changes do you see in him from Picture #1?____

____

____

____

How old do you think he is? ________________

How does this little boy feel?________________________

____

____

Do you feel drawn to him or would you avoid picking him up? ____

____

____

What do his hands tell you?_________________________

____

____

How old do you think he is?___________________

How would you describe this young boy? ____________

____

____

____

Would you say he is content and happy? ____________

____

____

____

How old do you think he is?____________________

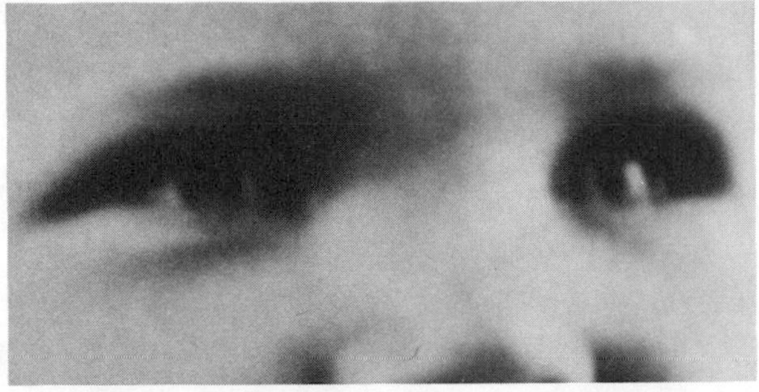

Without the rest of the picture to influence you, study only his eyes. Write the words that you think describe how this baby feels. ____________________

____

____

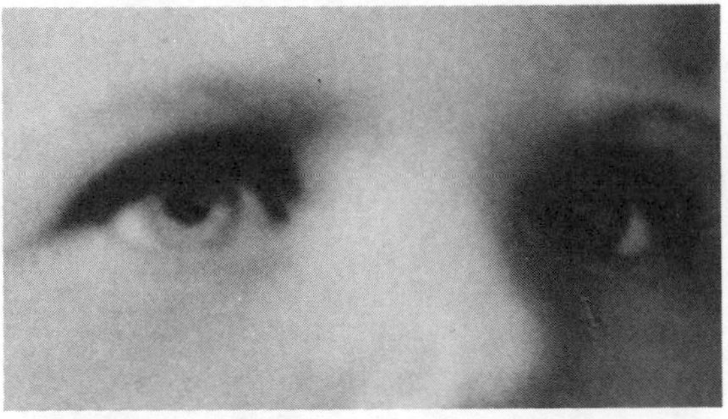

Study only his eyes. Write the words that you think describe how this baby feels. ____________________

____

____

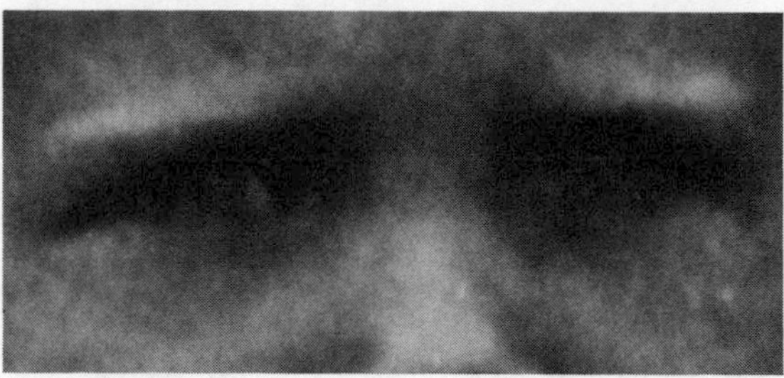

Looking at just the eyes of the little boy on the pony, what do you see?____________________________________

____

____

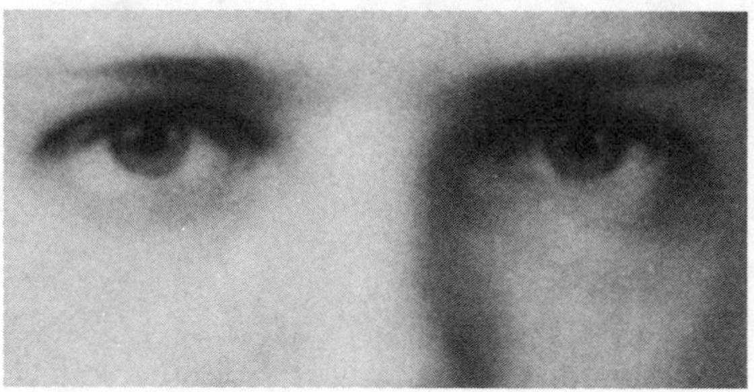

Do you see anything in this teenager's eyes that you didn't see before? _________ Look carefully. Describe what you see in him: ________________________________

____

____

As you may have noticed, these four pictures are the same person at different stages in his life. You may even have guessed the identity of this person. These photographs are of me. The pictures tell a powerful tale and are very revealing when carefully studied. Looking at them will help you read your own pictures.

Picture #1 is little baby Fred, probably at the age of ten months. Everything about the picture, the smile, the look in the eyes, the secure grasp of the chair by the left hand and the comfortable position of the right hand on his leg, indicates a normal, healthy and happy child. He feels secure in himself and about himself. This is the way a young child should look and feel about himself.

Picture #2 appears to be a little boy suddenly turned very serious and, perhaps, a little sad. The picture is clearly a photograph taken in a studio. He has on a pretty suit with a lace collar. His hair has been properly prepared for the picture. His right hand is again resting on his leg but in a very different position. We might describe it as flat or emotionless. Significant? It might be. We wonder, does he look sad because he has to pose so long in a studio and really doesn't want his picture taken? Or is there something else? My mother's handwriting on the back of the picture reads: *Fred, Jr., age 2 years and 4 months.*

Picture #3: Little Fred is neither comfortable nor happy sitting on this pony. His hands are not on the reins. In fact, he looks very insecure. Where, we wonder, has the sparkle gone from what we saw in the first picture? Riding a pony should be a fun experience for a child. The look of sadness from the first picture has intensified. In my mother's handwriting again: *Fred J. Littauer, Jr., about 4 years old.*

Picture #4: Here young Fred is approaching his sixteenth birthday. This picture was taken for the high school yearbook. This clearly shows a teenager who is careful about his grooming and appearance. His hair is combed neatly and his necktie, shirt and suit coat are carefully coordinated. A pleasant touch of a smile and wide-open eyes complete the picture.

Picture #5: Looking at baby Fred's eyes alone, we see clarity and sparkle. There is bright attention to whatever has captured his eyes to make a good picture. The eyes agree with the complete Picture #1.

Picture #6: We see a very intense look in his eyes. We do not see sparkle or vitality. We do not see happiness or contentment. Looking carefully, one sees a penetrating look. Comparing this with Picture #2, we see that this is not a happy child, certainly not on that day!

Picture #7: The eyes are a little less clear, but upon careful examination a look of fear can be perceived. Is the little boy afraid of the pony or is there some deeper issue revealed in his eyes? The pony in Picture #3 appears to be very docile and sedate. Since we know the little boy grew into manhood with a lot of the Choleric personality (often fearless), he is unlikely to be afraid of a quiet pony.[1] Why such intense unhappiness in these two pictures? What might have caused the child to change from his earlier sparkling vitality and security?

Picture #8 once again shows a deep intensity in this teenage boy. For years, I saw nothing more in this picture than a pleasant, well-groomed teenager with strong, clear, piercing eyes. I had forgotten how this teenager always tried to fit in and overcompensated for his low sense of self-esteem.

I was to learn even more about what the pictures of my own eyes revealed. Look back at the picture of the little four-year-old boy on that docile Shetland pony, on page 00. How did you answer the questions under the picture?

When I showed various people this picture in the first editions of this book, I asked them, "How does this little boy feel?" Most people would say such things as, "He's upset," "He's troubled," "Something's bothering him." That's pretty well agreed upon. The answer to my next question, "Do you feel drawn to him, or would you avoid picking him up?" was surprising.

Some answered, "He's upset, he needs to be loved. I would pick him up and love him." I was completely unprepared for the vast majority of people, however, who responded, "No, he's upset, but I wouldn't want to pick him up."

They didn't know who the little boy was! But, I knew. That little four-year-old boy didn't understand why people shunned him. He didn't understand why people avoided picking him up and loving him. As an adult, I felt like someone stuck a dagger through my heart when people looked at this picture and said, "No, I wouldn't want to pick him up. Suddenly an avalanche of the old feelings of rejection surged through me. My emotions were so flushed, I could barely get the words out, "That picture is of me when I was four years old.

Then it all became so clear. When a little child has been violated, the scars often remain in his eyes and countenance. That pain and hurt tend to push people away at the very moment he desperately needs to be loved and accepted. He has no understanding of the emotional struggle that begins to rage within him. The more he craves attention and acceptance, the more other people, even children, are repelled by his unhealthy clamoring. Thus the downward spiral continues and the feelings become locked in. No wonder I walked into marriage with deep needs to be loved, and feelings of childhood rejection that I never understood until many years later.

It was not until about three years ago, when I was conducting a workshop on understanding and identifying emotional pains of the past at a Christian conference, that I saw something I had never seen before. As I was relaxing during a short break, I covered my face in the picture with a blank piece of paper, all except for the eyes. Suddenly I saw a piercing intensity I had never noticed before. I was riveted to what I saw and I didn't like it. I felt emotion within. I thought to myself, *If I were the father of a teenage girl I would not let her go out on a date with this boy.* I was afraid of what I saw in that teenager's eyes! This was *me* I was talking about!

After the workshop, I hurried to find Florence to show her my discovery. When I showed her the photo, emotion welled up in her and she said, "That's the look I've been trying to tell you about for years." I had never before understood when she told me about the "looks" I gave her—looks of disapproval, looks of anger, looks that made her feel threatened. Now I understood. I now saw that same look in my high school yearbook photograph. It had been there all the time. Now the confrontation aboard ship a year and a half earlier made even more sense. I could better understand why Florence and Marita had told me there was anger in me that I needed to do something about.

God had already been doing His transforming work in my life. Apparently this was the day He chose to allow me to see this in myself. I knew where the look came from. I had already become aware of the strong feelings of rejection, of the possibility of some emotional "kind" of interference in my childhood and definitely in my late teenage years. I had already become very knowledgeable about the whole subject of childhood sexual interference.

But I, who would have previously denied with absolute certainty the possibility of any form of sexual abuse in my childhood, had one more surprising revelation ahead of me.

Even though I had many symptoms of childhood interference (deeply buried anger, low sense of self-worth for which I generally overcompensated, and strong sexual compulsions since earliest teen years, if not before), I would never have attributed them to childhood trauma. Like most people, I just didn't know. I simply didn't understand.

But that has all changed. My eyes have been opened. I have seen lives devastated by childhood interference and rejection. I have also seen lives transformed by the cleansing and healing power of the Lord Jesus Christ. Mine is one of them.

A New Revelation

In September 1989, Florence and I were speaking in a church in Australia at a conference named after our book, *Freeing Your Mind From Memories That Bind.* It was late Saturday afternoon and the conference would soon be over. Florence was seated behind me on the slightly raised platform. I was sharing with the audience the value and importance of childhood pictures and what they might reveal.

I had in my hands two pictures of myself, at two and a half and at sixteen, and one of Florence at ten months. I held the pictures in my hand for the group to see: a bright, sparkling, eager and clearly Sanguine/Choleric picture of Florence, and a serious and sad-looking picture of myself. I commented that I saw sadness in my eyes and I wondered why. Virtually all my childhood pictures had that sad look and I was often crying in early family movies. I suggested that apparently even at two years old that little boy did not feel loved. I had often shared this before and sometimes I felt deep emotion as I confessed those feelings.

Seated directly in front of me were Laurence and his wife Vivian. I had already met Vivian the previous weekend at another conference. We had talked privately and she shared with me of the interference she had suffered as a child. When they arrived this Saturday morning, Vivian had introduced me to Laurence. He didn't seem particularly excited to be there, but he did come and actually seemed to enjoy the conference more as the day went on. We had chatted a couple of times during the breaks and they stayed the entire day.

On this Saturday afternoon, as I usually did, I handed the three pictures to the audience to pass around. Laurence, being directly in front of me, was the one to receive them. I went on speaking and paid no further attention to the pictures. Florence, seated behind me, watched Laurence as he first looked at the cute, sparkling picture of little baby Florence. He grinned and passed it on to Vivian. Next was my two-year-old picture. Florence told me later that he glanced at it, blanched and immediately passed it on to Vivian. He could not look at it. What, Florence wondered, could have caused such a visibly obvious emotional reaction from just looking at my childhood picture?

She did not have to wait long for the answer. About twenty minutes later I concluded the presentation and headed to the foyer to be available to any who might have questions or need personal help. Florence remained on the platform for the same purpose. Laurence came up to her immediately and stated clearly, "I know Fred was molested before that picture was taken!"

Florence was incredulous. How could this man, who had never met us before today, who lived halfway around the world and "down under," who was not even born when I was a child, make such a statement? He knew almost nothing about me. Florence's shocked expression caused him to explain.

He was, he confessed, a convicted child molester. He had been in prison four times and became a Christian during his last jail term. He told Florence that whenever the uncontrollable urge came over him, he always looked for a child who had already been molested: "They're much easier to get to."

He admitted to molesting about one hundred little boys and girls in his lifetime. In simple terms, he was an expert. He could quickly spot a child who had already been interfered with. When he looked at two-year-old Fred, he said he could tell I had been molested. No wonder he had blanched at that picture. No wonder he had a strong emotional reaction. Now I began to have one as well.

Later, Laurence asked me if there was any chance he could meet with me before we flew home. We made an appointment to meet at the airport on the following Tuesday. Just as planned, Laurence and Vivian met us and we were able to find a quiet, secluded spot where we could talk privately. Before you judge Laurence too harshly—and the crimes he committed can in no way be condoned—you need to hear his own childhood horror story.

At the age of three, Laurence's alcoholic father disappeared. His mother, unable to keep Laurence, gave him to her sister to raise—immediate abandonment and rejection feelings for the little boy. When Laurence was about five, his cousin, then almost fifteen, began violating him violently, under threat. Finally, at about seven, when Laurence was not able to bear it any longer, he got up the courage to go to his aunt (who was now his stepmother) and tell her what her son was doing to him.

Tears came to Laurence's eyes as he told us how his aunt viciously beat him for telling such lies about her son. Now totally defenseless and without any protection, his hopeless plight continued for six years. At about the age of thirteen, Laurence ran away and for many years lived on the streets. As he grew older he began reenacting the crimes that were committed against him and a vicious cycle not only was maintained, it was multiplied in expanding rings, like the rings a pebble creates when thrown into a pond.

Needless to say, his prison terms neither helped him, cured him nor even gave him tools to enable him to handle his uncontrollable compulsions. We spent an hour and a half together that afternoon, and I reinforced in his mind the name of the only one who could help him, and what he must do in order to "come to Him" for his own healing and cleansing.

After Laurence dropped his bombshell, I began to pray and ask the Lord to show me what had happened to me so long ago. I remembered a live-in housekeeper, who came over from Germany in 1931, and who had immediately found employment with our family. She lived with us for twenty years. I had ample opportunity to know her well. As I look back on what I remember about her now, I clearly see the profile of a victim. I believe that the real reason she left Germany was to escape the abuse that may have been going on in her own life. She died many years ago in a psychiatric hospital.

There was no question in my mind that our housekeeper was the perpetrator. I wanted to know facts. A lot of healing had already taken place in my life and emotions, but since I was frequently speaking publicly about my own experiences, I didn't want to say, "I think I was violated myself." I wanted to know. I wanted to be sure. I wanted to be completely credible.

No matter how much or long I asked, I seemed to get nothing but brief flashes. Finally, a year and a half later, Florence and I were flying home through the night over the Pacific Ocean on Qantas Airlines, having completed another ministry trip to Australia. After sleeping a few hours, I awakened and once more began to ask the Lord to show me what this woman had done to me. Instead of answering my prayer, the Lord clearly showed me a man. Then I knew there was not just one, but two perpetrators. As I continued to ask the Lord to show me details, He did reveal to me who it was: my elementary shcool principal. Then I remembered. He was removed during my third grade year as principal, and the word homosexual came to my mind. A third grade boy could not have understood what that word meant.

This was such a surprise to me because my elementary school memories were so clear, I thought. Then I remembered that this principal was the director of a day camp that I went to one summer between second and third grade. I asked the Lord to take me back there as a child. Even with Forence praying with me, all I ever saw was pulling into the driveway, getting out of the car, and going up to the gate. I have no other memories of that day camp. In the weeks that followed, I could get no further knowledge of either violation. Yet I knew both were there. In addition, I had now identified ten clear symptoms of victimization in myself.

Finally, I called Sandy, whose own story is told in the next chapter. She was already serving as a prayer director in our ministry, and had helped many others uncover their buried memories. Since the Lord had used me to help Sandy uncover her victimization, it was only natural that I call her for help. We made an appointment to meet and pray together over the phone.

Florence and I were in a hotel in Houston, Sandy at home in California. I had to have the room very dark, any light was distracting. As soon as we both prayed and asked the Lord to reveal truth, I clearly could see myself standing in the middle of the housekeeper's bedroom. I could see exactly what I was wearing: a light blue cotton shirt and shorts suit, with buttons that attached the shorts to the shirt.

Then I could see her bed. She was lying on it, naked. I was instructed to get up on the bed. As that little two-and-a-half-year-old boy climbed up on the foot of the bed, a wave of audible emotion erupted from me. I clearly saw the violation that was done to me. A little boy was damaged, almost for life, but for the intervention and healing of the Lord.

I am certain these acts continued for several years, perhaps until I was about seven or eight, because I had no memories of those years of my childhood at home. For me this was a significant breakthrough. It helped explain many things. Digging up these roots expedited my healing process.

But what about the prinicpal? That was still unexplained. Once again I called Sandy. Nothing was coming through my personal prayer for memory retrieval. Now, three months later, I drove up to meet Sandy and her husband, Kevin. After dinner, the three of us went up to my hotel room to ask the Lord to fulfill His promise—"Ye shall know the truth." It was only seconds after we all had prayed that I saw myself standing in the principal's office. The door was closed. I could see his desk, his chair. There was no one in it. I looked around the room. Then I saw him. He was standing near the door in his three-piece suit. I saw that his pants were open, my right hand was clearly on him. I saw everything that happened. I was eight years old.

How could I have so totally repressed this memory? At that age I should have conscious knowledge of it. But even though I had only sight memory—whereas some people have memories that involve feeling, smell, and even sound—there was no question that this was real. I had had such clear memories of that school, my teachers, myself, even the school office, but I had no "memory" of the principal's office. I still cannot "see" where it is. One day I will go back to Henry Barnard School in New Rochelle, NY, and validate that memory.

Just as Laurence in Australia had learned to recognize vulnerability in little children, this principal must have also recognized the hurt that was in me from the violations that had taken place in my home. I lived for sixty-two years before I ever had any clear knowledge of the root of the struggles that had kept me in emotional bondage for so many years.

Before I uncovered my own victimization, God had already done much healing in my life, but it was nothing compared to the changes that have taken place since my memory retrievals. I am truly a different person today. All the old issues of rejection are fully gone. I am able to love my wife of now over forty years, and to be loved back as well, in a way that I would never have imagined before. Sometimes I hear her say the same kinds of things she would say years ago that made me feel so hurt and unappreciated. Today, those offhand remarks hold no pain or reaction for me. I have realized that the issues were not in what she was saying, but how I was receiving them.

I continue to come to the Lord daily in written prayer; I call it my communion with Him. I have realized that healing is not an event, it is a process, and He Himself promised to complete the work that He has begun in me. Is it any wonder that I want for you to receive that same healing from Him?

WARNING

The next two chapters contain the true stories of Sandy and Kevin, a fine Christian couple who were struggling with problems stemming from unidentified traumas in their past. With their permission I have shared explicit details—not for sensationalistic reasons but to illustrate the depths of despair from which God has set them free. I am sorry to report that their stories are not unlike hundreds of others I have heard.

If you sense that the explicit nature of their situations will offend you, please skip these chapters.

12

SANDY'S STORY

I met Sandy when she had traveled quite a distance to come to one of our CLASS seminars. I noticed her even before she asked if she could meet with me. There was pain in her eyes, a downcast look. Although she was clearly a committed believer, there was no joy, no sparkle, no bounce in her step. She could easily have been wearing a sign that said: *Trauma Within!*

She asked to see me because of the deep depression she had been in. She said it started in her teenage years. A number of times she had been to a psychiatrist who had diagnosed her as having a biochemical imbalance and put her on medication. She had been on the medication for five years but it didn't seem to help much. She was still depressed, and was also having sexual problems with her husband.

I first asked her if there was any possibility of sexual interference in her childhood. Sandy is among the one out of three who is aware. She answered yes; she had been abused by the husband of her mother's best friend.

"Sometimes the two mothers would go out and he would take care of me and his stepdaughter, Paula," Sandy related. "I remember one night when I was sleeping with my friend at their house. I woke up to find him standing by my bed rubbing me. He said he was checking to see if we were okay, but that's the only thing I remember."

Our available time that day was short. We had to move along quickly. Experience had shown me that this incident was probably not the whole story, and though possible, it was probably not the cause of a lifetime of depression. Very likely there was more.

Sandy was a sweet, attractive woman of thirty-five, desperate for help. The survey she took showed not only many symptoms, but also that she was aware of the molestation. She had never told anyone about it, nor in her counseling had anyone asked her.

One of the things that facilitates our counseling at our seminars is that we're from out of town. Those who come to us think they will never see us again, so it's safe to be vulnerable and honest. I told her, "Sandy, I believe there may be more than you are aware of. But in order to confirm it quickly, I would need to ask you a few very personal and intimate questions. Would that be all right?"

Sandy said, "Yes, ask me anything if you think it will help. I can't live with this any longer."

I then proceeded to ask her the very personal but standard questions I have learned to ask of every man or woman who comes to me for help and whose survey scores indicate a clear possibility of childhood trauma. From Sandy's answers it was clear that the known molestation was only the tip of the iceberg.

I reviewed with Sandy some basic Scripture truths. Jesus has promised that she has a right to know the truth (John 8:32); the Holy Spirit has the power and ability to bring all things to her remembrance (John 14:26) and to guide her into all truth (John 16:13); and there is nothing covered that will not be revealed and hidden that will not be known and come to light (Matthew 10:26, Luke 8:17). I told Sandy there were three things she needed to do in order for God to reveal truth to her.

First, we must have a desire to find the truth and uncover the locked-away memories that have been suppressed. God is not likely to force us to see that which we do not want to face. Not only is the desire essential, we must also be willing, without reservation or restriction, to see truth, no matter upon whose shoulders the guilt or responsibility falls. It could be, in fact often is, someone whom we hold in the highest regard. If God wants for us to see that such a person may be involved, we must not only acknowledge that possibility, but also be willing to know. For some, this is the most difficult step. But God has made it possible for us to handle that:

> No temptation [trial or testing] has overtaken you but such as is common to man; and God is faithful, who will not allow you to be tempted beyond what you are able; but with the temptation will provide the way of escape also, that you may be able to endure it (1 Corinthians 10:13, NASB).

Second, we must believe. We must believe that God, through His Holy Spirit, has the ability to unlock that strongbox of memories that we had securely padlocked so many years ago. And in order to believe that He has that ability, we must first believe that He is: "I *will* deliver thee . . . saith the Lord . . . I *will surely deliver thee* . . . because thou hast put thy trust in Me, saith the Lord" (Jeremiah 39:17,18). If you have never trusted your life to Him, if you have not received Him as your Savior and Lord, you have no foundation to believe He has the ability to do anything.

Do you know God personally? If you are not sure, or if you are not sure He knows you, carefully read, "How to Know God Personally" in Part IV. Sandy did believe, and she was ready for the third step.

Third, we must ask. We have to come to Him in prayer and ask Him to reveal whatever we need to see from our childhood. Sandy was ready. I asked her to pray aloud, claiming God's promises of Scripture and asking Him to reveal that which was hidden. She did just that. I then followed her in prayer, agreeing with her and in support of her, bringing her needs to our Father.

A Faith-Building Experience

Immediately following our prayer, intense emotions began welling up from the depth of Sandy's being. The memory came flooding upon her almost immediately.

She was lying in bed in her friend Paula's room. Paula's stepfather came into the room and over to the bed. She not only sensed his presence but could feel his hand on her. She rolled away from him toward the wall, trying to get away, hoping he would leave her alone. She did not scream out. That was significant.

I encouraged her to allow God to reveal whatever else might be there to see. Sandy was sobbing. "He's pulling me back. He's getting on top of me. He's trying to get in me. Oh, he is!"

Sandy had seen enough for this moment. I asked her to open her tear-filled eyes. She had actually seen, even re-experienced, the childhood rape that had been locked away. Gradually Sandy's emotions quieted down and we were able to talk about what the Lord had allowed her to see, memories of which she had absolutely no conscious knowledge.

She had wanted to know the truth. She had asked the Lord. He answered her prayer almost instantly. What a faith builder that is, to pray to an unseen God and to have Him immediately give you visible evidence of His answer. It was visible to Sandy because she could see in her mind's eye what had actually happened. It was visible to me because I could see the physical manifestation as the tears came pouring out. The reality of the violation resulted in natural and obvious grief.

I asked Sandy the question that is so important to ask any person who has just discovered suppressed victimization. "Sandy, was what you just saw real or imaginary?"

In Sandy's case, it was all too real. "Oh, yes, it was real." There was no question in her mind that the memories that burst forth in answer to her prayers had been an actual experience from her childhood. To others who have gone through similar memory retrieval, such an incident often seems to be so implausible that it must be imagination. Never in their conscious minds has any such occurrence been even a remote possibility. Therefore, when the memory is retrieved, they feel it can't be real. While the emotions are remembering and reacting to the traumatic experience, the mind does not want to believe or accept it and begins a work of denial. Many victims will feel the tug, a war going on between their emotions and their mind.

At this point I asked Sandy, "Did you pray and ask God to reveal truth to you?"

"Yes."

"Is God a deceiver? Is He the Father of lies? Would He lie to you when you asked Him to show you truth?"

"No."

"Who is the deceiver? Who would want you to think that what you just saw and experienced was nothing more than your imagination?"

"Satan."

"Exactly! Was that real or did you imagine it?"

"It was real!"

Even though Sandy knew it was real, it was important for her to confirm for herself that God had revealed truth to her. And she was not just remembering a childhood experience as an adult. She was reliving that childhood trauma as a little child. She didn't say, "I remember him pulling me back." What she did say was, "He's pulling me back." That thirty-year-old incident was being re-enacted in the mind and emotions of a little child.

Satan Doesn't Want to Let Go

It was important for Sandy to be certain that it was God's Holy Spirit who had unlocked her padlocked memory box. It is Satan who doesn't want her to see truth or to dig up the root of her adult depression and other problems. Satan wants to keep her in confusion, doubt and turmoil. Even a child of God who is depressed and downcast cannot glorify her Father in Heaven, cannot effectively bear fruit for Him in the area of ministry to which she has been called. The enemy has her in his camp and he has no intention of releasing her.

I prepared Sandy to realize that the next morning she would likely be tested with doubts and confusion. Sandy needed to be able to sort out truth from fantasy. She needed to be able to stand securely on the knowledge that she had in fact prayed to God, that she had asked Him to reveal truth and that He had answered her prayer. He had allowed her to see and experience an actual event from her childhood. With this security, she was armed to fend off the fiery darts of confusion from the evil one.

As Sandy's emotions of pain subsided, they were replaced by feelings of thanksgiving. Thanksgiving? Is it possible that she could be thankful for what she had just seen from her childhood? I asked Sandy how she felt. Her response: "Relieved."

All her life Sandy had been in turmoil. There were things she just didn't understand. Her life, her marriage or her feelings were not going the way she had believed they would. Depression and despair overshadowed the joy and peace she knew were promised her as a Christian. Now, suddenly, it all began to fit together. Things that didn't make sense before were becoming clear. She felt relieved and thankful. The veil that had covered her life for thirty years had been torn in two. The Lord had unlocked the gates that imprisoned her for many years in bondage. This was the beginning of liberation. Ahead, the work of restoration, the journey of cleansing and healing.

Now for the first time in her life, in response to her prayer, her heavenly Father had dug up the root of her problems and brought it to the light. Her psychiatrist, she said, had only cut down the weeds by prescribing medication to lift her out of her depression. He had never gotten to the root of her problems. He had never asked the right questions. On all her visits over several years, he had only asked general questions about how she was feeling in order to determine the types and quantities of medication to give her. He was practicing psycho-pharmacology, treating emotional manifestations with medication, controlling but never curing the problems, treating the fruit without treating the root. Cutting back the weeds merely removes them temporarily from our sight. In time the weeds grow back and once more have to be cut down.

It is not until we dig up the roots of the weeds that we can have a beautiful lawn. God wants us to dig up the sin in our life. We must not only confess the sins we have committed, but we must also dig up the sins that were committed against us. That day Sandy was ready and willing, and under the guidance of the Holy Spirit she dug up the sin buried inside the tent of her mind.

When the Going Gets Tough

A couple of months later, Sandy and her husband Kevin came to a Freeing Your Mind conference we were conducting in a city near their home. I met Kevin for the first time. He was, as Sandy had told me, both supportive and understanding of Sandy's search for wholeness.

Kevin was in his late thirties, attractive, tall and muscular. More important, he was a deeply committed Christian, and both he and Sandy were active in the ministry of their church. Since there were about three hundred people at the conference, we had little time for more than greetings and a brief reunion.

Two and a half weeks later, I received a call from Sandy. She said she had "shut down" after the conference and was struggling. Last Saturday she had gotten very ill, exactly ten years to the day she had been told she had cancer. Yesterday had been an extremely bad day emotionally—she couldn't stop crying. In her own words, she felt "spiritually, physically and emotionally dismantled." She couldn't seem to pray for herself. Even writing her prayers, which I had urged her to do several months before, had been especially hard.

Since the conference she had experienced a number of flashbacks.

One, when she was about eight, of her older brother holding her nose and mouth.

Another of him, nude and in an aroused state, coming after her in the living room while she was hiding behind the couch.

Another, when she was ten or eleven, of being put in a big corrugated box with a friend by some older neighbor boys and being told they had to do whatever the boys said.

And another, of looking inside the front door of a friend's house which was all black inside. All she could see was the end of a sofa with a man on it, telling her to come in.

Finally, just a few nights before her call, her husband had been hugging and kissing her when she suddenly "felt trapped and had to push away."

"Intellectually," Sandy told me, "I know the power of the Lord and the blood of Christ, but right now it doesn't feel real to me." She asked me if we could have a meeting over the telephone. She felt there was more to dig up and she wanted to get out whatever the Lord wanted for her to see. But she hesitated. "If we find more, will it be as painful as the first time?" She wanted to dig out all the weeds that were necessary but she didn't know if she could handle any more pain.

I asked her, "Sandy, have you ever had a splinter in your finger that was buried in your skin?"

I remember that myself very clearly as a little boy. My mother would get a needle and sanitize it over the open flame on the kitchen stove. Then she would dig into my skin, cutting it and pulling it apart, to get to the splinter.

I can still feel the sharp pain as the needle poked around in the tender flesh and touched the splinter, working at it to dig it out. Mother would squeeze my finger tightly to help deaden the hurt. Finally, relief came when the splinter was removed from its hiding place. Mother held it triumphantly on the end of the needle for me to examine. The pain of the digging was the worst. My finger felt so good when the splinter was finally out. The swelling would go down and the wound would soon heal. So it is when we dig out emotional splinters. There is often sharp emotional pain when traumatic memories are dug out.

I explained to Sandy that the child could not emotionally handle the pain, but God, in His infinite wisdom, had provided a means for the child to put aside both the memory and the pain until some later time when as an adult she would be able to bear it. Very often, the pain that was buried as a child still needs to be felt as an adult.

I reminded her of our Lord's words:

> Truly, truly, I say unto you, that you will weep and lament . . . you will be sorrowful, but your sorrow will be turned to joy. Whenever a woman is in travail she has sorrow, because her hour has come; but when she gives birth to the child, she remembers the anguish no more, for joy that a child has been born into the world (John 16:20,21, NASB).

"Sandy," I gently told her, "that is the way it is with digging out the emotional splinters that have been festering for so long in us. Some people experience much pain and some experience little pain. Sexual interference affects each one of us differently. Once it is out, however, the cleansing and healing begin."

We made plans for her to call me one month later at 6 P.M. I asked if Kevin could be available that evening for comfort and support if needed. Sandy assured me that Kevin would be with her.

What a blessing it was to know that Sandy had a husband who was supportive and understanding and who was willing to be at her side in the event he was needed. Not every wife is so fortunate. Too often we hear of husbands who are impatient or disinterested in their wives' emotional struggles.

We have found that often a husband who is impatient or dogmatic about his wife's feelings may very likely be suppressing hurts from his own childhood. It is a fact that emotionally hurting people are attracted to other people with similar levels of emotional pain. Victims tend to marry victims. A husband tries to escape from his own feelings by having a negative attitude toward his wife's. For those who think that they are in this situation, we highly recommend the only resource we know of that deals with this issue, the book *When Victims Marry* by Don and Jan Frank (Here's Life Publishers).

I had one more recommendation for Sandy. I reminded her of the importance of spending time daily in written prayer. Not only is this a powerful part of God's promise of restoration, but it also lays a strong foundation in asking Him to help us retrieve more lost memories.

A Divine Appointment

One month later, right at 6 P.M., the phone rang. It was Sandy, as scheduled. Kevin was there on the other phone, available to be a comforter to his wife. None of us had any idea at the moment what the Lord would reveal this night. This proved to be an ordained appointment.

As Sandy and I began talking, she remembered that two weeks after our first meeting during the CLASS seminar, she woke up three nights in a row choking. She couldn't breathe. Somehow the name of her brother Stan came to her mind.

She remembered how people used to say how much Stan loved his younger sister Karen, and that he used to take her on long walks. I asked Sandy about Karen's life today. Sandy described her as very insecure, with a poor self-image. I asked her if she thought there was any possibility of abuse in Karen's childhood. "Well, I've wondered about that, possibly by Stan," Sandy admitted.

I then asked about other siblings. "I have one other sister, Allison, a year younger than Karen."

"How would you describe her life emotionally today?"

"She's already been in drug rehabilitation for cocaine. She's in counseling now, and I think she's in denial."

This was not a pretty picture of a healthy American family. At the earlier meeting we had found severe abuse in Sandy's life. I had suspected that what we found then was not the only incident. There were two significant keys. One, she thought she was probably about ten years old and, two, as I reminded her at a later time, she had done nothing to resist her little friend's stepfather. She hadn't even screamed. Most sexual abuse of little girls takes place between the ages of three and five and a girl at the age of ten who has not been pre-conditioned by earlier abuse is much more likely to resist and even fight back. Her natural defense mechanisms have not been broken down. But Sandy had not resisted. She had not screamed. It was as if she simply had accepted the inevitable.

What might have happened to Sandy previously? Why did she feel she had no choice but to do as she was told? Where would we begin to look in her memory bank to find other and earlier instances of abuse?

I looked over the list of flashbacks she had described to me that had occurred after the Freeing Your Mind seminar. There were two that immediately stood out as particularly significant: Her brother Stan coming after her in the living room, and the partial picture of a sofa with a man on it in an otherwise black house. Any home or room that is black is invariably a sign that memories have been shut off or blanked out. I thought either one of these memories would be a place to start.

After about a half hour of general questioning, I felt it was time to ask the Lord to do His work, to reopen Sandy's locked box of lost memories. I invited Sandy to pray first, and I followed her. This time, though, there was no flood of emotion. Nothing was happening.

Sometimes the Process Is Difficult

I said to her, "Sandy, with your eyes shut to blank out any distractions in your room, I want you to go back to your house in Delaware where you lived until you were eight years old. I want you to try to find a little girl there, a little girl about four, five or six, a little girl named Sandy. I want you to try to see yourself as a little child in that house. When you do, I want you to tell me where you are. We are not trying to *remember* anything. I just want you to try to find yourself somewhere in that house."

I waited. Nothing happened. No response came across the telephone lines. I asked again, "Sandy, can you see anything? Can you find yourself in your house?"

For some people this is very difficult. For others it comes readily. If the individual has reasonably clear memories of the inside of the house, finding himself in it is much easier. However, we have seen many instances of people who, with seemingly no knowledge of the inside of a childhood home, find a shred of a picture which then becomes clearer and clearer.

Finally, Sandy replied, "I can't find myself at all." This was not to be the relatively quick re-enactment at our first meeting. The living room became the first place to look—the living room that appeared in the flashback with her brother Stan, who is almost nine years older than Sandy. I asked her, "Sandy, can you see the living room of your house?"

In a moment she replied, "Oh, yes, I can see the living room quite clearly."

"Tell me, what you can see in the living room. Can you see a couch?"

"Yes, I can see it."

"Look behind the couch, can you see anything there?"

"Yes, I'm hiding there, crouched in the corner."

"Sandy, I want you to look around the room from where you are hiding. Is there anybody else in the room? Can you see anyone?"

"Yes, I can see my brother."

"Look at him carefully. What is he wearing?"

"He's not wearing anything. He's nude."

"Now, look at him again. Is there anything you notice about him?"

"Yes, he's aroused."

"Sandy, how do you feel as you crouch in the corner?"

"I'm scared. I'm afraid he might find me."

"Sandy, look at him again. Is he coming toward you?"

"Yes, but I don't want him to. I don't want him to find me."

"Sandy, where is your brother now?"

"He's standing right in front of me. He's laughing at me. I don't want to look at him. I'm afraid."

"Sandy, is he reaching down for you?"

"I don't want him to. I don't want him to get me."

"Is he touching you?"

"I don't know. I want to run away!"

At this point Sandy began to fight the memory. The fear indicated her emotions were beginning to remember what her mind had forgotten and did not want to see. At this point, many times the victim will say, "I got up and ran out of the room."

This usually means they don't want to see anything else. At that point, then, I gently say, "No, I don't think the scene is over yet. I think there is more God wants you to see. I want you to come back and crouch down in that corner again." The victim has been taught to do what they are told, so they will usually return and the scene recommences.

During this entire time, Sandy, and every other person who seeks Holy Spirit-guided memory retrieval, is fully awake, and cognizant of the conversation taking place. Afterwards she will remember everything she has said. This is completely different from hypnosis, in which the patient's mind is in the control of another person, and afterwards the patient will have no knowledge of anything that was revealed. I personally do not feel hypnosis is appropriate for a Christian. The work of the Holy Spirit is accurate, reliable, quicker and never revealed in secret. I would rather be guided by the Holy Spirit than in the control of a hypnotist.

Sandy did not try to run away; neither did she want to see what was happening. I had to say to her, "Sandy, I think your brother is trying to reach for your hand. If he does, I want you to let him."

Immediately came her reply, "He's got me by my arm, but I won't go." As the scene further unfolded, Sandy's brother Stan literally dragged her out from behind the couch.

"Sandy, how old are you?"

With hardly a hesitation, she said, "I'm about six."

"Sandy, what are you wearing?"

"A little white dress with ruffles."

Since Sandy was about six, Stan was close to fifteen. After dragging Sandy out from behind the couch, Stan picked her up and carried her out of the living room, down the hall and into his room.

At this point, stop and reflect: Why was Sandy afraid? Why was she crouching in hiding behind the couch? We can be fairly certain that the rest of the scene which is about to unfold was not the first such incident.

Suddenly little Sandy was standing all alone in Stan's room. "Where is Stan?"

"I don't see him, he's gone."

"Sandy, look back at the door. Is it open or is it closed?"

"It's closed."

"Can you see Stan's bed?"

"Yes."

"Is it made or unmade?"

"It's unmade."

"Where is Stan?"

"I don't know. I can't see him."

"Sandy, I want you to walk over to the bed. Can you do that?"

"Yes."

"I want you to climb up on the bed now. Can you do that?"

"Yes."

"Where are you now?"

"I'm sitting on the bed."

"Sandy, I'd like you to lie down on the bed. Can you do that?"

"Yes, I'm lying down."

"Now, Sandy, I want you to look around carefully on the bed. Is there anybody on the bed with you?"

In a moment Sandy replied, "Yes, he's lying next to me."

"What is he wearing?"

"Nothing."

"What do you notice about him?"

Stan had pulled little Sandy over to him, made her bend down over him and, holding her head in his hands, had forced her to give him oral sex. This little six-year-old child had been violated by the brother she should have been able to trust.

Sandy was sobbing now. She had not wanted to believe her brother might have done anything to her. Since this was her second memory retrieval, she knew it was real.

I asked over the phone, "Kevin, are you still there?" He answered that he was. "I think you had better go in and comfort Sandy." Sandy continued to sob. She had a right to grieve. She had a right to be angry at the sin that had been committed against her young body and mind, at the "defilement of her flesh and spirit" (2 Corinthians 7:1).

I asked Sandy to open her eyes as both Kevin and I tried to comfort and minister to her. As Sandy's emotions calmed down, we later talked about the man on the couch in her friend's house. She was too fragile and exhausted at this point to want to face that issue, but she did say in a very clear voice, "I'm sure he raped me, but I don't want to see it."

Sandy, as a child, was clearly a victim of multiple violations. No wonder she was subject to depression, downcast looks and sexual dysfunction in her marriage. Then Sandy asked me a question which surprised me . . . just a little. "Do you think there's any possibility of anything in Kevin's childhood?"

13

KEVIN'S STORY

Up to this point in our phone conversation, Sandy's husband Kevin had been supportive but mostly quiet. Now Sandy was asking me about him.

"Do you think there's any possibility of anything in Kevin's childhood?" she asked. "He's very afraid of the dark, and he has a terrible anger. He sometimes has a violent reaction to even imaginary things." As an afterthought she added, "Oh, and he's always been afraid of dogs!"

Kevin, you'll remember, is big, tall and muscular. Afraid of the dark? And of dogs? And subject to violent reactions?

Kevin promptly echoed, "Fred, do you think you would have time to work with me?" Knowing that victims tend to marry victims, and that these were no insignificant symptoms, I agreed. Something, somewhere, must have happened.

At 7:20 that same evening our focus shifted to Kevin. Sandy was now calm and in God's care. Her mind turned from her own hurts to the symptoms of her loving and supportive husband. There might even be hidden explanations for his care and sensitivity. She waited in curious anticipation of what the Lord might reveal from Kevin's childhood.

Kevin and I began looking for clues that would show us where to search, where the Holy Spirit should shine His light. Kevin had been raised in Indiana and had lived in the same house from about age one to eighteen. His memories of his childhood home were both clear and positive. There appeared to be no dark spots.

Summer vacations were spent camping with his family. He remembered those vacations with enthusiasm: "They were a very positive experience. I loved to go camping with my father. I do remember, though, even as a teenager, being very concerned when I had to go to the outhouse at night. I was scared to go alone."

Sandy interjected, "Tell Fred about the time you were working for the extermination company in Arizona and almost killed your boss. Fred, he has violent reactions to unexpected things, even to imaginary things."

"It was summer time," Kevin began, "and I had arrived at this house to do my regular service call. There were two guys sitting on the porch. They kept staring at me. One of them kept looking at my pants. I knew these guys were gay. They kept trying to get me to come in the house and have a drink. I wasn't about to go in that house with them. When I had to service the inside, I told them to stay on the porch, and I meant it! I would have killed them if they had come near me.

"While working in the back by the swimming pool, the special drill bit I was using broke. I went back to my truck and looked in my tool box for another. They kept watching me the whole time. I couldn't find one so I had to call the office to have someone bring another out so I could finish the job. I returned to my work in the back. I was so intent on what I was doing, I didn't hear my boss approaching. He tapped me on the shoulder. I whirled around and almost killed him with the broken drill bit I had in my hands before I realized it was my boss."

This was surely a violent reaction to the unexpected. It suggested something, somewhere, but it didn't shed any particular light at this point. His strong feelings directed toward the two men on the porch also had roots somewhere.

I asked Kevin about his violent reaction to "even imaginary things." He replied, "Well, sometimes I think about the young man who will one day marry my daughter. I am going to meet with him before they get married. I will make very clear to him that if he *ever* beats my daughter, I will kill him!"

Kevin was not kidding. The emotion in his voice showed he meant every word of it.

Recurring Bad Dreams

I next asked Kevin about any recurring bad dreams he had, especially as a child. Dreams are, very often, keys to identifying the hidden emotions and experiences that may have produced the present fears, rages and reactions. Kevin told me of a dream he had recently. "I was in jail due to back taxes. Someone was trying to get me to do oral sex on him."

Then he remembered that one night when he was about six or seven, he was having problems sleeping. He got out of bed and went down to the living room where his parents were watching the late news on television. "They were showing a picture of a man that was wanted for murder. That really scared me. I was afraid he might come and get me. I don't know why I was so scared. My parents were both home and all the doors were locked."

Then he remembered that even as late as seventh grade he was afraid to take out the trash at night. There was no street light by their house.

Kevin told me that when he was about eleven his fourteen-year-old brother had tried to sodomize him: "We were both undressed and aroused. We hadn't a clue in the world what to do. I was lying on the carpet, face down. I saw him doing things to himself. My brother now has two sons himself, eleven and twelve. They're not doing well in school and have severe emotional problems. Recently, one of them was lying down in school curled up in the fetal position! I wonder if he has done anything to them."

It would appear that Kevin's brother may well have had serious sexual compulsions, but he was not the issue tonight. This experience with his brother may or may not have been particularly significant for Kevin. It might have been nothing more than a pre-teen experimenting and becoming familiar with his developing sexuality. His remark, "We didn't have a clue," would tend to indicate that.

Searching for negative feelings or unusual experiences in Kevin's childhood, we ran through his grade school years and teachers' names. He had both clear and good memories of each year. When he came to third grade, Mrs. Morrison's class, he suddenly remembered that a friend of hers came to the Halloween party dressed as a witch. "It freaked me out. I tried to kill her!" He then remembered that on Halloween night he absolutely would not go up to those houses that didn't have a porch light on.

Kevin then told me that at this same time, he had a friend who lived across the street on the corner. He didn't like his friend's older brother, who was about fourteen. They were a weird family: "I didn't like to go over there. They used to have knife fights on the lawn. I was frightened. I was in their house only once, during the day and just for a minute. One day the older brothers beat me up on the way home from school. When my father came home from work, he asked me what happened. I was afraid to tell him because they might do it again. When I told my father he said, 'C'mon with me.' I was scared of that whole family. I didn't want to go. He went over alone and called the boys' father outside. They had a fight. When my father came home he said to me, 'If they ever touch you again, you let me know.' They never did. My father was my hero. I always felt safe with him."

This boy loved and respected his father. There was no negative image here. More than a half hour had passed, and we had found nothing that seemed to be a clear clue to explain Kevin's powerful adult fears and violent reactions. There was no question that he had strong symptoms of sexual interference in early childhood. Intense fear of the dark, violent reactions, very strong feelings against homosexuals, the jail dream, compassion for those abused and fear of dogs (but so far no clues to that).

Though we only had a few symptoms, I felt they must have a root somewhere. Kevin's home life appeared to be well-balanced and positive. He seemed to have a good relationship with his father. His brother? There might be a possibility of something there, but somehow I didn't sense that was the issue.

Two People Know the Truth

Finally, I said, "Kevin, you have many significant symptoms of possible sexual abuse in your childhood. Frankly, nothing we have talked about tonight gives me any sense of where or when something might have happened, yet I strongly suspect it is there. I think it is time to ask the Holy Spirit to do His work. I think it is time for us both to pray and ask Him to bring to your remembrance [John 14:26] anything He wants for you to see. I don't know what might have happened to you. But there are two people who do know. Who are they?"

Without a moment's hesitation, Kevin answered, "Me and God."

"That's right! You don't remember, but He was there with you all the time, and He alone has the power to reveal to you that which has been hidden. In fact, He has promised in Matthew 10:26 to do that for you. Would you like to ask Him to do that?"

"Yes."

"Then you pray first, asking God to guide you into all truth, and I will follow you."

I had seen God do these kinds of miracles so many times. I knew He could do it for Kevin. I have seen Him take an unknowing adult back into a lost childhood experience, into the very room at the very time the violation was committed. Hadn't He done this twice already for Sandy?

Somehow Kevin's picture was too blind, too opaque, too clueless. I truly did not know where to begin. Kevin prayed over the telephone and then I prayed. I confessed that I had no idea where to begin. I prayed, "Lord, we are going to totally trust in You because we have no wisdom as to where to look. We ask You to reveal to Kevin that place and time in his childhood where something might have happened to him."

After we had both prayed aloud, I said, "Kevin, we don't know where to look, but we have asked the Lord to show you. I want you to shut your eyes and allow your mind to wander back into your childhood. I want you to try to find yourself somewhere as a little boy, wherever the Lord might take you, and when you find yourself, I want you to tell me."

We didn't have to spend hours or even many minutes searching through childhood homes, visiting room after room, probing for fear, insecurity or blackness, as with many other seekers of truth. Less than a minute passed when Kevin answered. What follows here are the exact words that Kevin spoke to me over the phone, in his normal adult voice and in his normal adult mind and understanding, but reliving a hurt of a three-year-old boy.

"I think I see myself—on my property. I'm behind the carport. It was before my dad built the garage. I'm standing beside a chain link fence. I'm feeling some fear. I've lost that little boy."

"Kevin, just relax and see if you can find that little boy again."

"I can see the boy hanging on to the chain link fence . . . I am that little boy!"

"Kevin, how old are you?"

"Three, maybe four."

"What are you wearing? Can you tell?"

"I have tennis shoes on, jeans and a plaid shirt. Oh, God, a dog came up—a big dog. He scared me, and I'm backing up. The dog came at me at the fence. I backed up four or five steps into someone or something behind me. I'm resting against his legs. He reached down and picked me up. He's carrying me into the house. I think it's my dad. I'm having trouble deciding what is truth and what is fantasy."

"Kevin, don't try to figure out what is happening. Just allow God to reveal truth to you."

It seemed we were getting very close to something. I did not expect Kevin's father to be involved. Kevin continued:

"I think I'm seeing parts of two separate incidents. I think it's my Uncle Bill—when he picks me up I'm not afraid anymore."

"Was it a big man?"

"Yes."

"Is your dad tall?"

"Yes."

The feelings of safety and security indicated he might have been seeing parts of two separate incidents. There was enough, however, with the dog and the fear to warrant a second look, a return to the start of the scene.

"Kevin, I want you to try to go back to the fence. Let's start all over."

"I think I'm there. Someone is pressing against me, on my buttocks and my back."

"How do you feel?"

"Annoyed. Oh, God, I'm turned around! Somebody's got me by the shoulders. Someone stuck a penis in my mouth!"

"Are you choking?"

"Yeah."

"Is he holding your head?"

"Yeah, his hand's on the back of my head. I bit him. He ran away. He ran by the shed."

"One of the kids from across the street?"

"Yeah, it might have been. He stopped and looked at me. His penis was out."

"Kevin, I want you to look at him carefully. Tell me what you see."

"He's about 5' 6", 135 pounds. He has a brown plaid shirt on, tan pants, brown shoes, like Hushpuppies. I think it was the father! That's who it was, the father of the boys!"

"Kevin, you can open your eyes now."

"I already have!"

"Have you ever seen that picture before?"

"No, never! It was weird. He turned me around and I couldn't see his face. If I had seen that, I would have told my dad."

After we talked some more about what Kevin had experienced, I asked him, "Was that real or did you imagine it?"

"Oh, it was real all right!"

Once again, God had demonstrated His miraculous power. In our mortal wisdom, neither Kevin nor I had any idea of what might have happened to him or where any incident might have taken place. Only God in His sovereign righteousness answered our prayers and immediately took Kevin to the place and the time in his childhood when and where he was victimized! It was no wonder that he had a gripping fear of the dark and of dogs, and it certainly explained the recurring bad dream and his violent attitude toward homosexuals. Even his anger and violent reactions were now explainable. He had a right to his anger. He had a right to be angry at the sin that was committed against him. A sin of which for thirty-five years he had no knowledge. A great God had answered his prayer and given him the knowledge he had asked for.

Liberated From Fear

Kevin need live in fear no more. God has given him the step of liberation. He has been released from the bondage of his emotions. For both Kevin and Sandy the *work* of restoration is still ahead of them.

That Wednesday evening, the three of us spent two and a half hours together on the phone. The Lord was there the whole time. He had given a powerful victory to Kevin and Sandy; two awesome demonstrations of His power and ability, His unique character that "passeth human understanding."

Kevin's last words to me on the phone that night were, "Fred, you have an incredible ministry." As I recalled Kevin's words later, I looked back at my own written prayers for that day. The Lord had recently given me Acts 26:18. I wondered, could it possibly have been the same day? I looked in my prayer book for that day. I had written this verse that morning:

> I am sending thee, to open their eyes and to turn them from darkness to light, and from the power of Satan unto God, that they may receive . . . [their] inheritance among them which are sanctified by faith that is in me (NASB).

The Christian life is a constant and continuing journey into wholeness and into holiness: "He who began a good work in you will perfect it until the day of Christ Jesus" (Philippians 1:6, NASB).

Sandy and Kevin are one more example of the valid axiom, victims tend to marry victims. When they met and married, neither had any awareness of the nature or extent of their childhood sexual violations, in either their own or in each other's lives. Sandy had only the awareness of some minor molestation. Even though each one had no adult knowledge whatsoever, both had been traumatically, orally violated in early childhood. In Sandy's life, the first violation set the stage for the several that followed.

For Sandy and Kevin, their journey of restoration had taken a measurable step forward. They would be able to experience the reality of God's promise:

> I am the Lord your God . . . I have broken the bands of your yoke, and made you go upright (Leviticus 26:13).

They would be better able to replace the yoke of emotional bondage with the yoke of their Lord Jesus Christ.

> *Come to Me,* all who are weary and heavy laden, and I will give you rest. *Take my yoke* upon you, and *learn from Me* . . . and you shall find rest for your souls (Matthew 11:28,29, NASB).

14

GUIDELINES FOR MEMORY RETRIEVAL

Memory retrieval is the rediscovering of experiences we endured in childhood which were too painful to accept as reality at the time. They were then either consciously or unconsciously suppressed deep within our memory bank.

There is obviously no need to find every childhood memory that has lapsed into obscurity. Our minds would be cluttered with useless trivia. It is only when there are adult issues which are troubling us that we need to dig up certain specific roots in order to free our abundant green lawn from the weeds sown by the enemy.

Flashbacks May Be an Early Clue

As you read, study and allow your mind to ponder on the experiences of others, you may find reactions and feelings in yourself that surprise you, that you don't understand. You may find bits and pieces of a picture flashing in your mind. These momentary scenes are known as *flashbacks.* They may be just a few pieces connected together like a jigsaw puzzle, clear in the center but hazy or jagged on the edges. Until you commenced your search, you may not have given more than a passing thought to these flashbacks. Suddenly you sense there may be some significance to these pictures—and there probably is. They are likely to be a minute part of a long-suppressed early childhood trauma.

If you have been having flashbacks, you might want to write down in a journal a description of everything you see, even if it doesn't seem to make any sense. Also write down any feelings or emotions that are connected with what you see. We refer to this as *journaling*. It is a healthy practice that helps bring these experiences, emotions and feelings into a clearer light. Carry your journal with you. Write in it each time you have flashbacks or feelings. You may amaze yourself at the documentary of yourself you are developing. (Please note: A journal is totally different from a prayer notebook, and it is recommended that you keep them completely separate.)

Another suggestion: When flashbacks do occur, try to keep the picture "on the screen" of your mind. Avoid shutting it off. Keep your mind focused on it. It may become larger and clearer. It may develop much like a Polaroid picture does, slowly becoming clearer. It may develop movement. Or it may move from one frame to another like a film. If the flashback is ugly or frightening, it will not be easy to continue to watch it.

About a year ago I started working with Janet when she called our office after reading *Freeing Your Mind From Memories That Bind*. After listening to her pain and suffering, it was clear she needed help. She had a long list of symptoms but no knowledge of any interference. We made an appointment for a Holy Spirit guided-memory retrieval over the telephone for a few weeks later.

In answer to Janet's prayers, the Holy Spirit brought back several clear instances of tragic sexual interference on the farm where she had lived as a child. Both her father and a farm hand were identified. In addition, she saw the long-lost memory and experienced the pain of her father locking her in a big barrel. Several months later I met Janet for the first time when I was speaking at a church not far from her home, and we spent over an hour together. I encouraged her to continue on the healing journey and we prayed together.

Recently, Janet called again. This time she shared some concerns she was feeling and we talked about the implications. Almost matter-of-factly, Janet mentioned that lately she had been having mental pictures of someone throwing a baby into a flaming furnace. It seemed to be her father. She never saw the baby, nor could she tell who it was. It was just a mental picture. She hadn't spent a lot of time thinking about it. It was too ugly and too strange.

Knowing Janet and her background as I did, I felt sure it was not fantasy. It was strange and it was ugly. At this point in Janet's journey it seemed to be a clue to something still uncovered. My mind focused on a horrible new dimension of childhood devastation that I had been learning more about in recent months—something I had only heard about before.

If in fact, as a child, Janet had witnessed such an unbelievable crime, what could it mean? Janet is not a flighty person, subject to vain imaginations. She is a sensible, mature Christian woman who has dedicated her life to help and comfort other hurting women. The flashback must be significant, especially in light of all the other uncovered trauma in her life.

This image appeared to have the earmarks of satanic ritualistic abuse, the most brutish form of destruction to children. I had recently learned from a friend who had been victimized by "satanic circumcision," the disfigurement of a little girl's body for purposes of marking the rites of the coven.

Two days later Janet called me back. She found the physical evidence on her body. Her flashback was real. It led Janet to further recovery of lost memories of her childhood, more trash to be taken out, more cleaning, more healing.

We know little about the prevalence of this form of abuse, except that it is more widespread than anyone could imagine. Gynecologists who knew what to look for could develop a statistical profile. In one three-month period I learned of four adult Christian women who had suffered this form of violation, and who had personally found the corroborating physical evidence.

During the past six months, the Lord has chosen to use me to assist ten women uncover ritualistic sexual violation in their very early childhood through Holy Spirit-guided memory retrieval.

In the section titled "Mental Flashes" from our book *Freeing Your Mind From Memories That Bind,* we tell the true story of Ira from Colorado who casually mentioned that he saw one picture in his mind, one mental flash, every day of his life. We felt that was significant. I asked Ira to describe it: "It's just a brief instant, and then it's gone; it's a dark, private part of a woman."

This flashback was the clue to a memory that was retrieved of a childhood molestation at the approximate age of three—a little boy whose adult life was devastated by a woman's compulsive cravings.

If you are willing, you can allow flashbacks to give you the clues to what you may be searching for. Not everyone has flashbacks. Many do not. They are important to memory retrieval. Think of them as early warning radar.

Take a Counselor Along

Before considering the concept of Holy Spirit-guided memory retrieval, it is most important to recognize that the discovery of such trauma can be emotionally devastating and very painful. We strongly recommend that you *never* attempt this alone. It should only be done with the aid of an experienced Christian counselor who understands the possible consequences from the discovery of traumatic childhood experiences. It is always our policy to have a mature third person present and available as both a prayer supporter and a comforter.

Your counselor may recommend the gradual peeling off of the layers until you reach the core of the problem. You should follow your counselor's guidance. However, once the probability of unknown interference has been identified, we feel there is both scriptural and emotional validity for quickly digging up the infected root:

> For the Word of God is quick, and powerful and sharper than any two-edged sword, piercing even to the dividing asunder of soul and spirit, and of the joints and marrow, and is a discerner of the thoughts and intents of the heart. . . . Let us therefore come boldly unto the throne of grace, that we may obtain mercy, and find grace in time of need (Hebrews 4:12,16).

Did not the Lord command Joshua to call out the tribes of Israel the very next morning after the presence of sin had been determined? And did not Joshua immediately send the messengers to Achan's tent to dig up that sin once the offense and the offender had been identified?

We have met many men and women who, in searching for the truth, have gradually peeled back layer upon layer without yet finding the root. Although they know it is there, they have struggled all this time with the frustration of not finding it, in addition to the stress, the strain and the symptoms which caused them to seek help in the first place. From our experience, the quicker the emotional cancer can be cut out, the better. *Awareness is the first step to freedom.*

Steps of Memory Retrieval

The three steps to memory retrieval are simple and easy to remember: D.B.A.—no longer willing to "**D**o **B**usiness **A**s" usual. Work through this section with your counselor so he or she can guide you and support you through this process. We've also included some help and guidelines for your counselor to follow as he works with you.

1. Desire

The Lord is a rewarder to those who diligently seek Him, to those who want to know the truth. But He never forces Himself upon us and will rarely force truth upon us. We must not only desire to know the truth, but we also must be willing to face the pain that the child could not endure. We must want to know the truth without reservation or restriction. We must be willing to accept the reality no matter upon whose shoulders the responsibility may fall. One woman, who clearly had some roots to dig up and who honestly wanted to know, ran into an impenetrable barrier when she expressed her fear, "I couldn't bear it if it was my father."

The Holy Spirit was able to take her right up to the point where apparent interference may have been committed, but she could go no further because she admitted she was "blocking." She was protecting her emotions from seeing that which she felt would be too painful to bear.

Before she could see the truth she would need to pray and ask the Lord to give her that which she lacked, a desire to know the truth. If you want to know, but are afraid of what or who the Holy Spirit might allow you to see, then begin praying for the desire to know the truth without reservation. When you have the desire you are ready to proceed.

2. Believe

Believe that He is . . . that He is the living God . . . and that He is able to come to the aid of those who come to Him.

> Without faith it is impossible to please Him, for he who comes to God *must believe* that He is and that He is a rewarder of those who seek Him (Hebrews 11:6, NASB).

> But let him ask in faith without any doubting for the one who doubts is like the surf of the sea driven and tossed by the wind. For let not that man expect that he will receive anything from the Lord (James 1:6, NASB).

He is the Living God. He is our Redeemer, our Everlasting Counselor. He will bring all things to our remembrance and will guide us into all truth. He is there for us. It is up to us to believe.

3. Ask

The third step is simply to ask. Ask the Lord to reveal to you whatever it is you need to see from your childhood. If you desire, if you believe and if you ask, He will answer:

> Keep asking and it shall be given to you; keep seeking and you shall find; keep knocking and it shall be opened to you. For every one who asks receives, and he who seeks finds; and to him who knocks it shall be opened. Or what man is there among you, when his son shall ask him for a loaf, will give him a stone? . . . If you . . . then . . . know how to give good gifts to your children, how much more shall your Father who is in heaven give what is good to those who ask Him? (Matthew 7:7-11, NASB)

If it is good for you to know, and if you have a right to know, your Father in heaven will reveal it to you—if you ask. He knows. He was there all the time. He knew you from the moment you were conceived in that secret place. He knows your comings and your goings. He knows every hair on your head. He knows your past and your present. He knows your future.

In the presence of your counselor, pray aloud a simple and sincere prayer. Ask the Lord to reveal anything you need to know from your childhood so you may be set free, released from the bands of your emotional bondage. Ask in faith, believing that He, and He alone, can reveal it to you.

The ways of the Lord are a mystery; we cannot understand. We do not need to understand. We simply need to obey and abide. For some, the answers take ten to fifteen minutes of probing and digging into childhood. For others, a laborious and lengthy digging is required. Do not be disheartened if your answer does not come at once. God is sovereign and He is omniscient. He knows what you can handle and when you can handle it. He never gives you more than you can bear or endure (1 Corinthians 10:13).

Guidance for the Counselor in Memory Retrieval

After the seeker of truth has prayed, we usually suggest that he (or she) sit back in the chair and relax. We ask him to shut his eyes, explaining this is only to blank out any distractions that might occur in the room. This enables him to keep his attention focused on wherever the Lord may take him, on whatever the Lord may reveal. Then we will ask, "The very first thing that the Lord shows to you, or the very first thing that comes to your mind, I want you to tell me what it is." (We have already determined from our earlier interview the nature of the suspected interference, and often times from understanding certain symptoms, the gender of the victimizer. Refer back to the chapter: "Tough Questions, Important Answers."

If after a minute or two nothing comes, we ask the person to try to find himself in a specific place: the barn, the front yard, in the house, the garage, etc.—any place that would help the adult find himself as a child. We remind him that we are not asking him to remember anything or any place, but simply to find himself as a child.

Once a location is set, we ask the person to look around: "Tell me what you see," always asking for more details, helping to make the scene clearer. "Is there anyone else with you? How do you feel?" If they answer "fine" or "okay," we move to another room, asking if they see a door.

We try to guide the victim under the leading of the Holy Spirit to the place of perpetration.

Shortly after one woman found herself in the barn with her cousins, she said, "Now I'm in my room."

"Is there anyone in the room with you?"

"Yes, my two cousins."

"Where are they?"

She went on to describe them, what they were wearing and what she was wearing. Within minutes she was able to accurately describe the sexual trauma to which she had been subjected.

Another woman immediately saw herself in the back yard of her grandfather's house at her own fifth birthday party. He was angry at her because she had stepped on one of his flowers. Within minutes the scene changed to his living room. He was in a chair. She was standing in the room. He called her over to him, scolded her for being bad and told her what she must do to make it right. Not only did he orally abuse her, he made her feel guilty and ashamed as though it were her fault. It was a scene she had never remembered before.

She felt all the pain the little child experienced when it happened. It was ugly and awful, but she felt released afterwards. She had dug up the root. She could now come to the Lord for her journey into complete restoration. In the process of the memory retrieval, she realized that the little girl had known what she must do for her grandfather. Thus the Lord allowed her to understand that this was not the first time an incident of this nature had happened.

It is continually amazing to us, even as many times as we have been used by the Lord to dig up rotting roots, how the Lord will take the adult back as a child to the place and the time where the victimization occurred. When we ask for truth, He helps us to find it.

Letting the Light of Jesus Shine in the Darkness

One of our most spiritually thrilling and faith-strengthening meetings happened just a few months ago. Through interview with Jenny, it was fairly evident what might have happened and where. After we both prayed, I asked her to try to find herself at the age of about five in her home in Texas.

She found herself easily in the kitchen. There was no problem there and I directed her to walk into all the rooms downstairs. Everything was fine. We went upstairs into the first bedroom, then into the bathroom. She had a fairly clear picture of both. Walking down the hall she came to a closed door. I asked her whose room it was. She replied, "My parents.'"

I asked her, "Is the door open or closed?"

"Closed."

"Can you see the doorknob?"

"Yes."

"Is it on the left or the right?"

"It's on the left."

"Can you reach it?"

"Yes."

"Can you open the door?"

"Yes."

"Okay, let's open the door. Is it open now?"

"Yes."

"Look in the room. Tell me what you see."

"I can't see anything. It's all black inside."

"Jenny, I want you to walk into that room."

"I can't. It's all black inside. I can't see anything. I'm afraid to go in."

"Jenny, you are sitting with me here in this office. It is safe for you to walk in there as a child. There is a floor in that room. You can walk into it. I want you to walk in there. You will be all right. Can you walk in there now?"

"Yes."

"Are you in there?"

"Yes."

"Tell me, Jenny, what do you see in there now?"

"I can't see anything. It's all black!"

"Jenny, can you see a window?" (From experience, I knew we could help a child see in the room by light that might be coming in a window.)

"No, I can't even see a window."

"Jenny, look down at your feet. Can you see your feet?"

"No, I can't see anything! Everything is black."

"Jenny, are you sure you are standing in that room?"

"Yes, I am."

The wisdom and experience the Lord had given me seemed to be of no avail here. We had done everything I knew to do except look for a light switch and turn it on. I was led to suggest to Jenny that she pray again. I reminded her that Jesus said, "I am the light of the world."

"Jenny, this room is totally black to you. There must be a reason you can't see anything. I want you to stop for a moment and pray out loud, asking the Lord Jesus to shine His light into that room so you can see whatever He wants you to see."

Jenny prayed as I suggested. After her prayer, ten—perhaps fifteen—seconds passed, when Jenny suddenly exclaimed, "There's light coming into the room. It's getting clearer."

I could hardly contain the spiritual emotion I was feeling. Jesus had shined His light into that black room so Jenny could see. I couldn't believe what I was hearing.

Well, yes I could, but what an incredible answer to prayer. He answered it instantly.

"The room is coming into focus!"

"Jenny, look around. Can you see anything now?"

"Yes, I can see a dresser over there, against the wall. And I see the window to the left behind it."

"Can you see a bed?"

"Yes, it's over here."

"Jenny, is there anyone in the room with you?"

"No, I don't see anyone. Oh, now I see my father."

"Where is he?"

"He's over by the chair next to the dresser."

"What is he wearing? Can you tell what he has on?"

"I see work pants, a shirt and suspenders."

"What is he doing now?"

"He's taking off his shirt."

It was only a short time before Jenny saw her father lying on the bed. The little girl walked over to the bed, reluctantly climbed up and sat on it. Minutes later Jenny re-experienced the interference as she was forced to fondle her father.

We cannot begin to comprehend in our human mind the awesome power of the Holy Spirit. In the past two years I have seen many amazing answers to prayer and my own faith has been richly strengthened again and again. To have Jesus shine His light into that black room to enable Jenny to retrieve her lost memories, who would believe? Only those who believe!

Fact or Fiction?

It is essential that the counselor or prayer director never put suggestions into the mind of the seeker. The revealing must come solely to the individual as the Holy Spirit guides her into all truth. Otherwise, as the victim contemplates later what has been revealed, the devil will confound her thinking with lies: "You never really saw that. Your counselor told you that happened." The seeds of doubt and confusion have been sown. The prayer director can lead, ask, encourage and even occasionally direct, but he should never tell the victim what is going to happen.

> There is nothing covered that will not be revealed and hidden that will not be known . . . and come to light (Matthew 10:26; Luke 8:17, NASB).

Desire, believe and ask—and it shall be made known to you!

The experiences of memory retrieval can be extremely different from person to person. The truth may come on instantly like a floodgate. Or much probing and digging may be required with the help of an experienced prayer director or counselor. Sometimes it is necessary to go step by step, room by room, bed by bed, until a place is found that is dark or scary, a place where the child is afraid or unwilling to go.

Sometimes we have to instruct the child to go where she doesn't want to go. For example, whenever a child on a bed is uncomfortable or afraid, we can feel we are close to the scene. We must remain in that scene, even when the child wants to leave or get down. The child does not want to have to endure the trauma again, even though it is unknown at the moment. But if there is to be release and freedom as the Lord has promised, the truth must be known.

Once a horrible memory has been uncovered and the truth known, it is important to determine if it was indeed truth or if it was fantasy. We ask the question, "Was what you just saw real, or did you imagine it?" Answers will range from, "That was real, all right," to "I'm not really sure," to "That couldn't possibly have happened, could it?" Then we need to review the process. Did we ask God for guidance? (We always pray aloud in support after the seeker prays.) Is He a deceiver? Is He the father of lies? Would He give a stone when you ask for bread, a lie when you ask for truth?

The answer is always no, but the deceiver himself will try to confound the truth, especially the next day. He does not want the victim released. He hates to see anyone on the road to cleansing and healing. He desperately wants to keep the victim in bondage. That is his whole mission. He will do everything in his power to confound the truth.

It's important to realize that memory retrieval involves the child *re-experiencing* the trauma, not simply the adult *remembering* it. No five-year-old child could imagine what the Holy Spirit reveals.

It is our job to confirm the truth when God reveals it.

> For our struggle is not against flesh and blood but against the rulers, against the powers, against the world forces of this darkness, against the spiritual forces of wickedness in the heavenly places (Ephesians 6:12, NASB).

The Beginning of Healing

Once the traumatic memory has been discovered, and we have ministered to the individual and his or her emotions, we are ready for the most traumatic and rewarding step in our healing process—asking the Lord Jesus to come into that place of pain and minister to the hurts of the child. For those who have never heard of such experiences, what you are about to read may be, at first, difficult to comprehend and accept.

First, we must go back to our authority, the Scripture itself. There are numerous accounts of the Lord's bodily appearances after the resurrection. Sometimes we tend to forget that these promises and truths are just as valid today as they were in Christ's own day. Because these truths may be outside of our own frame of reference, or the extent of our personal experience, we often doubt and question them. Here is one of many verses which states the promise: "... He who loves Me ... I too will love him and show Myself to him." (John 14:21 NIV)

While working with the victim, we ask the person if they would be willing to go back to their place of violation. To remove any doubts or fears, we assure them that nothing bad will happen—this will be a good experience. The victim is asked to close their eyes. We then pray and ask the Lord Jesus to remove the perpetrator or any bad persons from that place. Next, we ask the victim to return to that room. It is amazing how quickly they are now able to return.

"Are you back in that room?"

"Yes"

"Is there anyone else in there with You?" Generally, their answer is No. The room has been effectively cleared by the Holy Spirit. If the answer is Yes, we ask the child to turn around in that place, and once again we pray for the Lord to remove any persons from the room. Upon turning back, the room is invariably clear. Now we tell the victim that there is someone or something that they should see, something good. At this time we pray silently and ask the Lord to fulfill His promise of John 14:21. Or we simply ask Jesus to go into that place and minister to the victim.

We then ask the victim to look around and tell us what is in the room. It often happens that they immediately say "I see Jesus!" (Note that we have made no suggestive remarks that it is Jesus that they will see.) We then ask such questions as, "Where is He?" "What is he wearing?" Consistently the answer is, "a long bright white robe." (See Matt. 17. He usually manifests Himself exactly as He appeared to Peter, and James, and John on the Mount of Transfiguration!)

We then ask, "What is He doing?"

"He's reaching his hands out to me," is often the answer. We then encourage the child to go to Him. From this point on a ministry beautiful to behold takes place. We do nothing more than ask questions. "Is He saying anything to You?" "Is there anything you would like to ask Jesus?" "What is He doing now?" Invariably Jesus will pick-up the child and tell him or her, "It's okay," or "I love You." The adult, reporting through their eyes as a child will be able to clearly describe every aspect of this precious encounter. It is very rare that the child does not ever see Jesus. Occasionally, they may need a little help.

At one Promise of Healing workshop, after we had done a demonstration memory retrieval for the entire group, I asked the lady who was up front with me to shut her eyes again and return to "that room." She had no trouble getting back there. The room was empty, and remained empty even after several minutes. She could see nothing. I felt led, as I had done on some previous occasions, to ask her to look over to her left. "Do you see a light or a glow?"

She answered "Yes." I told her to focus on the glow. Soon it became a glowing light, then the form of a person. Then she responded, "It looks like Jesus." It was Jesus and He came to her and comforted her after a particularly devastating group violation took place in the temple of a secret brotherhood. He not only ministered to her hurt and pain, but after a time, He put her down and took her by the hand and walked with her out of that evil place.

Which of her hands did he hold as He walked out of there with her? He held her left hand, as he always does. He was holding her <u>in His right hand!</u> She was at the <u>right hand of the Lord!</u> We do not rush her out of this scene, but allow her to remain in the infinite physical presence of her Lord. When He is ready, He will take His leave of her. At that time she can open her eyes. The healing that the Lord Jesus gives during this time is, in a human sense, unquestionably amazing. It is a huge step forward in the healing journey.

After memory retrieval, it is always our practice to ask the Lord to come and personally minister to the child, to their hurt, shame, and guilt. Once the person has experienced the physical presence of Jesus, no one can snatch away that reality. No one can ever tell them that they never really saw Jesus. They did! Additionally, their faith has been enlarged forever. Imagine how it deepens the faith of the prayer director, as they participate in the beautiful restoration taking place right in front of them.

For most people, seeing Jesus in His divine bodily presence is a first time experience. We remind them of the passage in Matthew 17 on the Mount of Transfiguration. We share with them the aspects of their experience that are identical to what many others have seen. Upon completing our personal time of ministry to the individual, we remind them that healing of the emotional pain resulting from their victimization is not a one-time event, but a journey. It still is essential for them to come to the Lord Jesus daily in prayer according to Matthew 11:28 and the Lord's promise is to provide rest. He says "Come." If we do our part, He will do His. He will give. He alone can give that rest, the inner peace, that was stolen from us.

"Come to Me, all <u>you</u> who labor and are heavy laden, and I will give you rest." (Matt. 11:28)

Part III

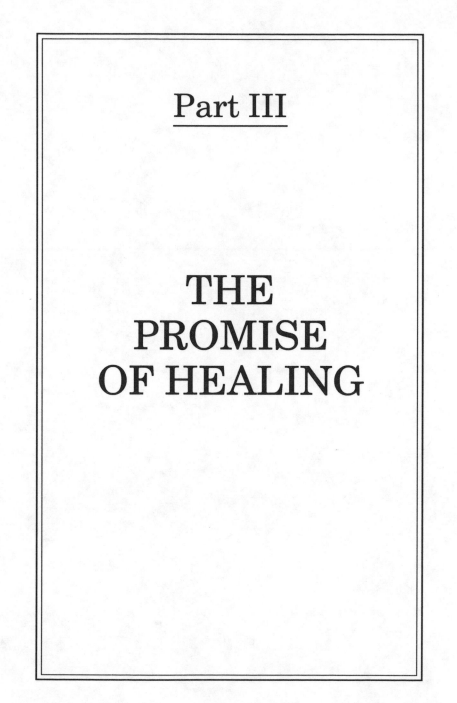

THE PROMISE OF HEALING

15

HIS PROMISES OF HEALING

Healing is not a secondary blessing. It is a vital part of Jesus' three-fold purpose expressed in Luke 4:18: to preach the good news to the poor; to proclaim freedom and release for the prisoners, the captives, the oppressed, those in bondage of any form; and healing, recovery of sight to the blind. His purpose may be described as salvation, liberation and restoration, all a part of God's plan of redemption.

His purpose is not to grant salvation to those who receive Him and then leave them in their same state of misery. Nor would He liberate those in bondage without granting forgiveness of their sins through His death on the cross. Nor did he come to heal their broken bodies and spirits only to allow them to die in sin and captivity. God's plan for man's redemption is complete. It only waits for us to act upon what He has already given us. We must respond to receive salvation. We must act to receive restoration.

Did He come to heal us of our emotional hurts and pain as well as our physical hurts and pain? By all means! The Scriptures make it very clear that He came to heal *all* manner of sickness and *all* manner of disease among the people (Matthew 4:23; 9:35):

> He healeth the broken in heart and bindeth up their wounds (Psalm 147:3).
>
> Bless the Lord, O my soul, and forget not *all* His benefits . . . who healeth *all* thy diseases (Psalm 103:2,3).

> I have seen his ways, and will heal him: I will lead him also, and restore comforts unto him and to his mourners. Peace to him that is far off, and to him that is near, saith the Lord; and I will heal him (Isaiah 57:18,19).

So often we think the Lord is only interested in physical wounds. To admit we might have emotional wounds somehow seems unspiritual. When we are already hurting, the last thing we want to do is put ourselves in a position where others might prejudge us.

To say, "I have a lot of anger in me that I can't get victory over"; or "My wife and I are really struggling. I don't understand her, and I don't think she's even trying to understand me"; or "I have just discovered I was molested when I was four years old. I'm falling apart. I don't know what to do!" puts us in a position of vulnerability. Are these the kind of things you could share in your church? Would you find compassion and understanding? Would you find help?

The Lord is interested in this kind of emotional pain. "He is?" you may ask. "Where does it say that in the Bible? How can I know He cares? How can I know He can heal these emotional hurts that I've struggled with for so long?"

Jesus understands suffering. He understands grief and sorrow. The Scriptures tell us He understands it well: "He is despised and rejected . . . a man of sorrows and acquainted with grief. . . . He hath borne our griefs, and carried our sorrows" (Isaiah 53:3,4). He carried them to the cross and through His suffering He confirmed our release and freedom "that through death He might render powerless . . . the devil; and might deliver those who . . . were subject to slavery [bondage] all their lives. He had to be made like His brethren in all things" (Hebrews 2:14-18, NASB).

Have you felt as though you have been in bondage? Are you now living in a situation that seems utterly hopeless? Are you sometimes so consumed with frustration that you simply give up? We have all had those feelings at some point in our life. You are not alone; nor, if you have Him, are you without hope. Our risen Savior understands our hopelessness. He knows how you feel and He is stretching His arms toward you now to help you:

> There is no creature hidden from His sight, but all things are open and laid bare to the eyes of Him. We do not have a high priest who cannot sympathize with our weaknesses, but one who has been tempted in all things as we are. . . . Let us therefore draw near with confidence . . . that we may receive mercy and find grace to help in time of need (Hebrews 4:13,15,16, NASB).

How do we receive His help, His healing? We must draw near to Him. We must come unto Him and He *will* give us rest for our weary soul. We must "draw nigh to God and He will draw nigh to you" (James 4:8).

He has promised, but we must act. We can no longer grant ourselves the deathly luxury of wallowing in self-pity, of saying life is hopeless. We must take the action that is necessary to come unto Him. His arms are now outstretched to you. You must take up His invitation and reach out to touch Him and receive His peace, the inner peace and rest He has promised.

What About Suffering?

There are two kinds of suffering you may be enduring. One is emotional and the other is physical. You may be living with a spouse who is emotionally or physically abusing you. It may be a parent or a child who treats you in a way that is completely disrespectful or abusive. You may have tolerated this treatment for a long time and given up. You may have lived this way for so long that you can't see any possible alternatives. If you are in this kind of situation, you are living in a dysfunctional home. Alcoholism, drugs, physical battering, rages of anger—these are only a few characteristics of a life that is out of control.

You may need to take some specific action to turn this situation around. We do not believe God intended, for example, for you to live with a husband who physically beats or sexually abuses you, or with a person who is continually emotionally abusive to you. God's Word assures us that "God is faithful . . . with the temptation [the trial, the testing] will provide the way of escape also, that you may be able to endure it" (1 Corinthians 10:13, NASB).

For some, the way of escape will be physical escape. Before taking this ultimate step, we strongly urge you to seek counsel. First, seek counsel from the everlasting Counselor, the Prince of Peace, through prayer. If you ask, He will answer. Second, obtain good Christian counsel from someone who can look at your situation and guide you objectively, scripturally and compassionately through the steps you need to take. In the words of Solomon, the wise counselor, "Where no counsel is, the people fall, but in the multitude of counselors there is safety. . . . he that hearkeneth unto counsel is wise" (Proverbs 11:14; 12:15).

Many of the poor choices we make in life are the result of our failure to seek counsel in the first place or to discount the recommendations that did not confirm what we already decided we wanted. Are you one of the thousands who made a lifetime commitment in choosing a mate against the counsel of family or friends, only to find out later you should have listened? Perhaps they saw something that you, in your haste to have your way, did not see or want to see.

Sometimes the way of escape may be to deal with the issue and face it head on. Don't ignore it or pretend it's not there and just hope one day it will go away. It was not easy for Florence and Marita to face me to tell me that there was anger in me that I needed to do something about. It was a monumental risk for them. They had no idea what my response would be. It could have been fearfully devastating. They had prayed and sought the mind of the Lord and felt they were in His will.

I didn't even know they were coming to see me! But the Lord knew. He had planned everything and orchestrated it. I needed to be reached. I am grateful today that they were willing to put their lives on the line for me, so manifold have His works been in our lives since then. Florence's decision and the action she took were the result of the safety she found in the wisdom of several counselors. In order to salvage her own emotions, life and marriage, something had to be done.

As I look back on all the suffering, frustration, pain of poor choices and hurt of rejection that I felt, and which I brought upon my family, I can clearly see how the Lord has used it all to strengthen me today. No one walks through the deep waters of life without being stronger once they reach the solid ground. We are then better prepared to ford that stream of turbulence if it ever races across our path again. It has rightly been said, "No pain, no gain." Even the Scripture says:

> We also exult in our tribulations, knowing that tribulation brings about perseverance; and perseverance, proven character; and proven character, hope; and hope does not disappoint; because the love of God has been poured out within our hearts through the Holy Spirit, who was given to us (Romans 5:3-5, NASB).

We are strengthened through our suffering; through it we learn obedience to God. When we obey, we are abiding in Him. When we abide in Him, we have inner peace despite our circumstances. This is the peace of God which guards our hearts and minds even when the world around us is collapsing. It is His gift to us (John 14:27). As I am learning obedience, the reality and depth of Scripture becomes more clear.

Jesus, our Lord and Savior, suffered emotionally and physically far more than we will ever be asked to suffer: "Although He was a Son, He learned obedience from the things which He suffered" (Hebrews 5:8, NASB).

Suffering, then, is often a part of our growth process. Its purpose may be to teach us the obedience and perseverance we need in order to become recipients of the healing He has promised. Healing is a journey during which the perseverance we have learned through obedience will serve us well.

His promise of healing requires both effort and action from us. We must come to Him, all ye who are brokenhearted, all ye who are weary and heavy laden, and He will give you rest for your soul.

No Sorrow I Can't Heal

by Jo Winkowitsch

Like a child who scrapes her knee,
I sometimes limp to God for love.
It feels so safe in my Father's arms
As He lifts me up above.

But though I need such comfort
I know I often run away . . .
Causing untreated wounds to hinder
What I think and do and say . . .

It's easier to cover up my sores
So none can see them bleed.
But then I miss such opportunities
To show how God can meet each need.

I will not market misery,
Or flaunt it for selfish gain.
But I have to find the balance
As I allow God to heal my pain.

Most of us have scars of suffering
And a cross that we must bear . . .
God's children are never left alone—
His comfort's always there!

Christ remains the perfect Band-Aid . . .
For He sees pain's shape and length.
Any injury will not destroy us
If we trust God's power and strength.

As I work through years of denial . . .
Toward what God wants me to be,
I must deal with the rancid heartache
Of the little girl who hides in me.

Freedom from dreams that torment
Is part of His miraculous goal . . .
If I depend on Christ completely,
His love will medicate my soul.

When memories hit my heart with hurt,
Christ knows just how I feel.
And throughout my life He's been whispering . . .
"You have *no sorrow* I can't heal."

16

IT'S AMAZING

Dear Fred,

I read *Freeing Your Mind From Memories That Bind* last summer and began praying that God would reveal to me the root of my anger. I have also had a difficult time feeling God's love, although I know in my head that He loves me. I attended my second CLASS in Phoenix in October. I had the opportunity to sit next to you at lunch and I shared with you how I was beginning a ministry for women with sexual trauma in their childhood. You told me about your survey and I asked for a copy.

When you gave it to me and asked me to fill it out, I was filled with fear. I knew it was something I had to do if I was ever to get any further in my relationship with God. Of course when I filled it out I had many clear signs of sexual trauma. You told me if I wanted to know, I could find out (a) if I wanted to, (b) if I wasn't protecting anyone and (c) if I would ask God. We made an appointment for the next day and you told me to spend time in prayer, asking God to open my mind to all truth.

It was a very distressing night. God slowly began to fill in a few pieces to this puzzle. The next day, after prayer and questioning, I remembered being molested by a babysitter's boyfriend when I was five (I don't believe it was the first time). Although I was afraid of finding out what was "wrong with me," it was freeing to know the truth. I have been angry ever since I was a child, and now I know why. I had come so far in my desire to know God intimately, but could go no further. I "disciplined" myself to study God's Word, but always found it hard to be consistent.

After finding the truth about myself, it was as though the Holy Spirit was unleashed in my life. I can't *not* study God's Word; I need to! I have an answer for the hope that is in me which I cannot help but share, and God has brought many people to me with whom I can share this hope. (I was paralyzed all my life in functioning as a servant for Christ. Now it is my passion!)

I have consistently kept my prayer journal, and God continues to teach me new things. I have also been very excited and challenged by reading *My Utmost For His Highest* [by Oswald Chambers]. There is tremendous depth and insight in this devotional. God's Word is now Jesus speaking to me personally and I finally feel like a new creature in Christ.

Throughout my life I have had trouble recalling Scripture that I had memorized. I find that my mind is clear now and verses that I memorized years ago readily come back to me. It's amazing!

Connie

Truly, the healing power of our God, the Lord Jesus Christ, is amazing. His way is simple. It is straight. It is light. It is we who complicate the issues. We mortals, having fallen to the pleasures of the world and the pressures of life, think there must be more to recovery and healing than simply coming to Jesus. But His offer to us always stands. It is everlasting and eternal. He simply said,

> *Come* to Me, all who are weary and heavy laden, and I will give you rest. *Take* my yoke upon you, and *learn* from Me, for I am gentle and humble in heart; and *You shall find rest for your souls* (Matthew 11:28,29, NASB).

Could anything be simpler? Are you weary and heavy laden? He promises rest for your weary soul.

There are some things we must do, some actions we must take in order to reap this promise. But He assures us: "My yoke is easy, and my load is light" (Matthew 11:30, NASB).

If His yoke is easy and His load is light, what are we waiting for? Let us come to Him!

The First Step to Healing

In light of this promise in Matthew, I have recently been studying the healings of Jesus recorded in the New Testament. It's fascinating to find that virtually everyone who desired healing came to Him. Either they came personally to Jesus, or a surrogate or an intercessor came on their behalf. Effort or action was required. They had to seek him out. They had to find Him, and come to Him—and He never turned any away!

It is interesting to note that with the few He chose to heal on His own initiative, it was almost always on the Sabbath and in the presence of the Pharisees. He chose to demonstrate the reality of His identity in this way to prove a point to the legalistic thinkers. Those healed were the unexpecting recipients of His mercy:

Matthew 12:10-13	The man with a withered hand—on the Sabbath, in the synagogue
Mark 1:23-28	The man with the unclean spirit—on the Sabbath, in the synagogue
Luke 13:10-13	The woman bent double—on the Sabbath, in the synagogue
Luke 14:2-4	The man suffering from dropsy—on the Sabbath, in the Pharisee's house
Luke 22:50-51	The ear of the slave at the betrayal—in the presence of the high priest
John 5:2-9	The paralytic at the pool of Bethesda—on the Sabbath

John 9:1-7	The blind man who washed in the pool of Siloam—on the Sabbath

Except for those seven, virtually all others *came to Jesus* for their healing. A few examples:

A leper *came to Him*	Matthew 8:2
A centurion *came to Him*	Matthew 8:5
They brought to Him many	Matthew 8:16
There arose a great storm . . . *they came*	Matthew 8:25
They *brought to Him* a paralytic	Matthew 9:2
A synagogue official named Jairus *came*	Matthew 9:18
A woman suffering from a hemorrhage *came*	Matthew 9:20
Two blind men followed Him, *crying out*	Matthew 9:27
A man demon-possessed was *brought to Him*	Matthew 9:32
At Gennesaret, *they brought to Him* all ill	Matthew 14:35
A Canaanite woman *came*	Matthew 15:22
Great multitudes *came, bringing* many others	Matthew 15:30
A man *came to Him* for his son	Matthew 17:14
Two blind men *cried out to Him*	Matthew 20:30

Shouldn't we also come to Jesus if we wish to be healed of the emotional pain that has festered in us? Many who came to Jesus for healing were willing to pay the price. They were willing, in many cases, to walk a long journey to find Him in order that they might come to Him. Our work today is not as difficult. We already know where to find Him. We do not have to search for Him. We only need to come to Him!

I am continually amazed to see how many people would rather pay enormous sums to spend one hour each week with a counselor, psychologist or psychiatrist, than spend one hour a day with Jesus at no material cost! Apparently we think that if we're paying a fee, something is happening. To come to Jesus for one hour a day must seem too intangible. We're not doing anything; we don't see any results. And yet it is He, and He alone, who has the power to heal.

Florence and I firmly believe in the value and help that Christian counselors and professionals offer to you. They have insight, understanding and wisdom that are extremely valuable. They may help you see things you can't see yourself. They can give you a plan for recovery and restoration. But what they cannot do is heal you! Healing is the province of the Lord, and for that we must come to Him.

The Work of Healing

We are already aware from 1 John 1:9 that He will "cleanse us from all unrighteousness." A significant verse in 2 Corinthians 7:1 tells us that we have an important role to perform in our own healing: "Let us cleanse ourselves from *all* defilement of flesh [body] and spirit [emotions]" (NASB). If we wish to be cleansed and healed from the defilement of our own bodies and emotions rooted in childhood interference, we must get busy in our own work of cleansing. There is a partnership required: "If we . . . then He." This is further confirmed in 1 John 3:3: "Every man that hath his hope in Him purifieth himself, even as He is pure."

And consider these verses:

> If a man therefore purge himself from these, he shall be a vessel unto honor, sanctified and meet for the Master's use, and prepared unto every good work (2 Timothy 2:21).
>
> Submit yourselves therefore to God . . . draw nigh to God and He will draw nigh to you. Cleanse your hands (James 4:7,8).

If we submit, draw nigh, confess, *then He* will draw nigh to us, cleanse us, heal us. The responsibility to follow through is on our shoulders. We must do our part if we expect Him to do His. If we fail to follow the directions He gives us, can we expect to reap the harvest?

His instructions might not always make sense to us. We don't have to understand; we must simply obey. In Luke 5, Jesus said to Simon Peter, "Put out into the deep water and let down your nets for a catch."

> Simon answered and said, "Master, we worked hard all night and caught nothing, but at your bidding I will let down the nets." And when they had done this, they enclosed a great quantity of fish (Luke 5:4-6, NASB).

Peter was obedient and did as the Lord directed. It didn't make any sense to him. He had already fished all night with no results. But without hesitation, he did his part, and then the Lord could fulfill His part. Simon reaped a rich harvest of blessings—so many that he had to summon his partners to help him!

Even in the unsought healing of the man with a withered hand, an effort was required in order for the man to receive what Jesus offered:

> He said to the man, "Stretch out your hand!" And he stretched it out, and it was restored to normal, like the other (Matthew 12:13, NASB).

We, too, must do our part as Jesus asks or directs. Then He will do His part!

What is our part? What must we do to be healed? We must ask ourselves, *How can I cleanse myself from the defilement of my flesh and spirit? How do I come to Him so that I may receive His rest?*

We believe the very best way to come to Him is in prayer. And, for most people, we believe the very best way to pray is using written prayer. Why written prayer?

Written Prayer

Written prayer is simply writing a letter each day to the Lord Jesus Christ. No special form, book or paper is required. Nobody is going to read over your prayer to see if you did it correctly. There will be no grades. How you do it is not important. Doing it is what's important!

Unfortunately, most Christians spend little time in prayer. We know it's good; we know we should; but somehow, with all the demands that are made on us each day, there never seems to be enough time.

Often when I meet with someone I ask, "How much time do you spend each day in prayer?" The most frequent answer I get is: "Not enough."

"How much is not enough?"

"Well, to tell you the truth, not very much at all!"

Another frequent response is, "Oh, I pray many times throughout the day."

"How long do you pray at each of those times?"

"Not very long. I tend to send up 'arrow' prayers."

Is this the kind of prayer the Lord wants from us? Is this the best we can give Him?

Prayer must be good for you, because it's so hard to do! With all the scriptural directives to pray, the many clear examples of the Lord Himself praying, the dozens of prayer seminars, the amount of prayer in church and prayer meetings, the pastor's preaching on prayer, why is it so many of us spend so little time in prayer?

In Luke 18, "He was telling them a parable to show that at all times *they ought to pray* and not to lose heart" (Luke 18:1, NASB).

Prayer had always been difficult for me. When I prayed alone, I found it hard to concentrate and stay alert, even to stay awake. Do you have trouble sleeping? Try praying! It's amazing how fast you may fall asleep! Bible study, on the other hand, has come comparatively easy for me. I have studied the Bible diligently for much of my Christian life. I have always enjoyed digging into the Scriptures, following a theme through cross-references, gleaning deeper truths and applying them to my daily personal and family experiences.

But prayer? That was a different story. I had tried everything I knew to do to make my personal prayer life vital. It rarely was. I would rise early in the morning and begin with study in the Word. Usually it was fruitful or meaningful, especially when I had a specific objective for the study. Then I would close my Bible, bow my head, shut my eyes and begin to pray. Invariably, one of three things would happen.

1. With my eyes closed, my mind would doze. Within minutes I might be in peaceful sleep, sitting up! It wasn't prayer, and if I wanted to sleep I could be much more comfortable back in bed!

2. I would begin in prayer and soon my mind would wander. All kinds of other thoughts would creep into my mind and I would suddenly become aware that I was thinking, but no longer praying. I never even knew when the transition took place; it was so subtle.

3. After beginning in prayer, I would realize that at some point my mind had jumped to the office, mentally organizing all the things I had to accomplish that day.

I also prayed beside my bed before going to sleep. But, since that seemed to be irregularly rewarding, such prayer was also irregular. This was especially true on nights when I was very tired, which was almost every night.

Many times I fell asleep in bed in the middle of one of my own sentences! Needless to say, none of this made for a very satisfying prayer experience.

To solve the problem of dozing off in the middle of silent prayer, I tried praying aloud. That seemed to work for a minute or two, and then one of those other factors switched into place. Without my being aware of it, my oral prayer would lapse into silent prayer, which then lapsed into dozing or mind wandering. Was it the enemy or was I just tired?

In short, I could never teach a prayer seminar or encourage or exhort another to pray because I could not share what I did not have.

That is all in the past now. Prayer has become the very foundation of my entire life. It is the single most important factor in my own journey of restoration. I am convinced it can be yours also.

Make a Habit of Meeting With God

Every morning I rise early and go to my desk. For both Florence and myself, our usual practice is to begin with a study and reading of Oswald Chambers's insightful *My Utmost for His Highest.* This devotional is one you can study over and over and the content continues to be relevant. It is always powerful because of Chambers's daily drumming into our minds that only in Jesus Christ can we find the answers to our human, emotional and spiritual needs. Even though he died before his fortieth birthday some seventy years ago, this book is regularly on today's bestseller lists. If you are not familiar with it, visit your Christian bookstore and purchase a copy. Don't miss it!

After a short reading for the day, I turn to the Scriptures. I may study around the verse in Chambers devotional. I may be meditatively studying through a Gospel or other book of the Bible. I may be doing research for a specific purpose. I may be reading through Psalms. I am always studying somewhere. God speaks to us through His Word. We block out most of God's communication to us if we are not studying. He also speaks to us when we pray, but most people who aren't studying are also not praying.

I have never been a proponent of the "three-chapters-a-day, check-it-off-my-chart" style of Bible reading. Careful studying, highlighting, underlining, note taking and writing in my own cross-references is much more productive for me. There is great spiritual exhilaration in mining the gold that is buried in the lode. I could not dig deep by giving several chapters a cursory once-over to satisfy my goal for the day. Such reading is certainly better than no reading, but for me it isn't the most satisfying.

Do whatever works best for you. The most important thing is that you do something! There are many good Bible study guides available at your Christian bookstore to help you in your quest for understanding God's Word.

Make Bible Study Uniquely Yours

The following letter arrived recently from Carol Barger of Phoenix, Arizona. She shared the results of her personal research in Psalms.

> Dear Florence,
>
> Thank you for sharing the depths of your heart with us at the Arizona Women's Retreat. The lessons, instructions and good humor are all powerful forces to move me to the next "pillar" in my service.
>
> I've enclosed two of my themes from reading through Psalms every month in 1989. When I came upon Psalm 104:24, "O Lord, how many are Thy works," I decided to list His works during my next reading through. I wanted specifics to mention in worship to Him and I discovered 252 specifics! Then I decided that I wanted to see the flipside of God's works—man's response. That's how "Bless the Lord" came about.

Carol

Shown below are just twenty-five of the 252 works Carol discovered in Psalms, with a few from Proverbs.

O Lord, How Many Are Thy Works

Psalm	**Lord, You . . .**
3	. . . are a shield about me, the One who lifts my head.
	. . . listen to me and sustain me.
4	. . . relieve my distress.
	. . . put gladness in my heart.
5	. . . bless the righteous man.
6	. . . hear and receive my prayers.
7	. . . judge the peoples.
	. . . save the upright in heart.
8	. . . displayed Thy splendor above the heavens.
	. . . created the heavens, moon, stars.
	. . . created man a little lower than God and crowned him with glory and honor.
	. . . put the creatures under man's authority.
	. . . rebuke the nations.
9	. . . destroy the wicked.
11	. . . test the righteous and the wicked.
13	. . . deal bountifully with me.
16	. . . counsel me.
Proverbs	
2	. . . reveal the path of life to me.
	. . . give wisdom, knowledge and understanding.
	. . . shield those who walk in integrity.
	. . . preserve the way of Your godly ones.
3	. . . reprove and discipline those You love.
	. . . founded the earth, established the heavens, broke up the deeps and sent the rain.
	. . . keep my foot from being caught.
	. . . give grace to the afflicted.

Having found so many nuggets as she dug deep into the Word, Carol then decided to record man's response to God's work and discovered 295 responses! We have listed the first twenty-five.

Bless the Lord, O My Soul

Psalm	
2:11	Worship the Lord with reverence; rejoice with trembling.
4:8	In peace I lie down and sleep for You alone, O Lord, do make me dwell in safety.
5:2	To Thee do I pray.
5:7	I will enter Your house and bow in reverence before You.
5:11	I sing for joy and exalt You.
8:3	I consider Your works and acknowledge, "How majestic is Your name in all the earth!"
9:1	Give thanks to the Lord with all my heart; tell of all Your wonders.
9:2	Be glad and exalt in You; sing praises to Your name.
9:11	Sing praises.
9:14	Rejoice in Your salvation.
11:1	Take refuge in the Lord.
11:7	Behold His face.
13:5	Trust in Thy lovingkindness.
16:8	Set the Lord continually before me.
16:9	My heart is glad, my flesh dwells securely.
17:6	I call upon You.
18:1	I love You.
18:6	I cry to my God for help.
18:23	I have kept myself from iniquity.
19:14	Let the words of my mouth and the meditations of my heart be acceptable in Your sight.
20:7	Boast in the name of the Lord.
21:13	Sing and praise Your power; tell of Your name, praise and stand in awe.
25:1	Lift up my soul to You, O Lord.

26:2 Examine me, try me, test my mind and heart.

26:7 I may proclaim with the voice of thanksgiving; declare Your wonders.

To fully appreciate the truths Carol has recorded, you might want to open your Bible to Psalms and Proverbs, locate and highlight each one, and use this as a guide to begin your own daily study in God's Word.

Develop Your Prayer Journal

Following my own study in the Word, I take up my prayer book. The most convenient format for me is an 8-1/2" x 11" spiral notebook. At the top of the page I write the day and the date and, since we travel so much, I record where I am—what city, airplane, hotel or church. Underneath I write the Scripture passages that I just studied. In the top right-hand corner of the page I write the number which represents how many consecutive days I have written my daily letter of communion to my Father in heaven. This is a new little detail I have added to help me with my discipline. I realized several months ago that because of my busy schedule, days would slip by when I hadn't managed to find time to come to the Lord. If I missed one day, it was not very hard to miss the next one. At times these lapses grew to four, five or six days.

I knew I needed a way to keep me accountable, for when I miss my visit with the Lord I become vulnerable to the "fiery darts of the evil one." Last November I started to keep a record of how many days I met with the Lord. It was eighteen days out of thirty. I couldn't believe I had missed that many! December was better—twenty-five of thirty-one. But January 1 started a new month and a new year and a chance to renew my commitment to daily prayer. I have to admit there have been a couple of times the Lord and I didn't meet until 11:45 P.M., but meet we did!

Now I try to make sure, no matter what my schedule, no matter how busy I am, to make time for the Lord. I never want to miss that special time that He and I have in my prayer closet. I can share with Him in secret and He rewards me openly. I commune with Him and, almost daily now, I hear from Him as well.

It is amazing what can happen when we get down to the serious business of prayer. When we come to the Lord, when we take His yoke upon us and learn from Him, He does give us the rest for our soul He promised (Matthew 11:28,29). My life has been completely changed because I have been faithful in coming to the Lord in daily, written prayer. And not only my life, but also the lives of everyone I know who regularly practices this daily communion.

The Power in Written Prayer

Last spring, after I spoke at one of our conferences, Janie waited until all the others had left the room. She had heard me speak on overcoming emotional pain through written prayer. Janie was a handsomely attractive woman, perfectly put together. She had a gentle air of confidence, and was clearly respected and well regarded by the other women. To look at her, immaculately dressed with a radiant countenance, one would presume she had overcome life's burdens and was living in peaceful and productive tranquility. But that, I discovered, was not the case.

As soon as we were alone, she poured out her feelings. She had been raised in a home where she felt she had been used by others. She now felt unloved and unappreciated by her husband. She felt he was so engulfed in his work that he was taking her for granted. She saw no hope in their high profile—but completely unsatisfactory—relationship. She was now in the later years of marriage—the years that should be rewarding but were not. In short, Janie was the image of perfection but was wearing a mask of peace to hide the pain that was raging underneath.

I couldn't solve her marital unhappiness in a few minutes. I didn't even know her husband. But I could give her some loving encouragement and some suggestions to help her deal with the deep-seated rejection and resentment she felt.

I urged Janie to begin writing her prayers. She had never heard of this before. I didn't urge her to try it; I urged her to *do* it as a daily practice. She had heard my experiences. She could see for herself the transformation God had worked in my life. When we left the room, Janie had a new hope and a determination to find healing for those old wounds. She knew God could change her attitudes and heal her hurts.

About four months later Janie called about the possibility of scheduling a conference. What we really talked about was the new Janie. Actually, I listened as Janie poured out the joy that was flooding her soul.

"Fred, I can't believe the changes that have taken place in me since I started writing my prayers. It's absolutely amazing! I feel like a new person. I spend at least one hour a day, and sometimes two, praying to the Lord. It's so exciting! He's doing so many new things with me and in me. Just last weekend I shared at our women's retreat that I had been writing my prayers. I told them what a blessing it is—how much closer the Lord and I have become to each other. So many of the women came up to talk to me afterwards. Fred, it's absolutely life changing!"

From the enthusiastic joy in her voice, I knew things must be much better at home as well. Janie is a new person because she has disciplined herself and her busy life. Besides being a wife and a mother, she is a speaker and a teacher. Janie made the time to spend daily with her Lord. The results have been awesome.

Janie is but one of countless men and women who daily reap the rich rewards of coming to the Lord in written prayer. Until you do it yourself, daily, you cannot comprehend its power. . . . It's amazing!

17

BENEFITS OF WRITTEN PRAYER

How can we hear the voice of the Lord if we are so caught up with our pressure-cooker lives that we leave no time to hear?

The idea of writing prayers is not new. It is, in fact, scriptural. We have an excellent example in the Bible of written prayers. If David hadn't written his pleas, hurts, needs and rejoicings to the Lord, we would not have the Psalms today.

Oswald Chambers wrote: "A most beneficial exercise in secret prayer before the Father, is to write things down so that I see exactly what I think and want to say. Only those who have tried these ways know the ineffable benefit of such times in secret."[1]

When we quietly take time to write our prayers to the Lord, we are also in a state of readiness to hear a word from the Lord. When the Lord does speak to us, we can immediately record in our prayer book what the Lord has said to us, even as He directed Jeremiah: "Write thee all the words that I have spoken unto thee in a book" (Jeremiah 30:2).

I do not mean to imply that everyone should write their prayers. I do, however, suggest that if your prayer life is not all you would like it to be or think it should be, you will undoubtedly find it a richer experience than you have ever thought possible.

Let us look at some blessings of written prayers.

1. It Prepares Us to Hear the Voice of the Lord

The Israelites sometimes heard the voice of the Lord as "powerful, full of majesty" (Psalm 29:4); at other times as "a still small voice" (1 Kings 19:12); but God always spoke clearly: "Thine ears shall hear a word behind thee saying, 'this is the way, walk ye in it.' . . . The Lord shall cause His glorious voice to be heard" (Isaiah 30:21,30).

But who will hear the voice of the Lord? Only those who are listening: "I have spoken unto them, but they have not heard . . . I have called unto them, but they have not answered" (Jeremiah 35:17).

2. It Enables Us to Fulfill Scripture in Our Lives

The Lord has given us commands, directions and instructions to enable us to take on His character, to become one with Him. As we've already seen, He instructs us to "come unto me, take my yoke upon you and learn from me." Writing our prayers on a daily basis enables us to come to Him. As we voluntarily take His yoke, lay it across our shoulders and walk down life's pathway with Him, we are submitted to Him. As we daily walk with Him, since He is the leader and the one with all knowledge, we learn from Him. He teaches us something new every day, that which He wants us to learn.

In John 15:4,5, the Lord tells us we must abide in Him, that apart from Him we can do nothing. What better way to fulfill this instruction than to come to Him daily in prayer? As we write our prayers, we are abiding in Him. Our attention is on the Lord Jesus Christ; our mind is stayed on Him.

3. It Fixes Our Focus on Him

"Thou wilt keep him in perfect peace whose mind is stayed on Thee" (Isaiah 26:3). Many people acknowledge that their minds have a tendency to wander while they pray. That is one way the enemy detours us from keeping our focus on the Lord.

If we write our prayers, on the other hand, we are able to concentrate more effectively. When we are writing, our pen stops if our mind wanders and this quickly alerts us to refocus on the Lord. Linda Setterberg, a mother of three small children in Fairbanks, Alaska, has been regularly writing prayers and says she is able to maintain her focus and pray even while watching her children. Carol Lewis of Houston, Texas, called recently to express the great chang- es in her life since she started writing her prayers: "It's been so exciting. I can't believe the change in my prayer life. I have been a Christian since I was twelve, but there always seemed to be something missing. Now there is such power in my life. In the past when I prayed, it was never more than five minutes, and my mind always had a tendency to wander. Just yesterday I prayed for three hours, and the day before for one hour. It is such a powerful experience."

Writing our prayers helps us maintain an undistracted focus of devotion. The resulting benefit is that the peace of God becomes a reality.

4. It Encourages Daily Discipline

Most of us need some form of help, especially when our lives are hectic and pressured, to bring us to our personal altar on a regular basis. How easy it is to miss a day here and there! The practice of dating our pages of prayers makes it pointedly clear when we have missed a day or two or three. We need that sense of discipline. We need a plan to help us maintain what we want to do. Resolutions are so easily made and broken.

I sometimes joke that running to airplanes is our only physical exercise. Recognizing that, I resolved in January to start a program of daily, brisk fifteen-minute walks. I did that successfully for about ten days before I missed one, then another and then another. That particular resolve needs to be totally reactivated. It has gone the way of most resolutions.

But I don't want to miss writing my prayers and spending time with the Lord in daily communion! In Matthew 6:33, we are instructed: "Seek ye first the kingdom of God, and His righteousness, and [then] all these things shall be added unto you." If we . . . then He! One of the clear implications of this verse is that He must be our first priority. We need the discipline of writing our prayers to keep Him first in our hearts.

5. It Establishes a Communion With God

Commune means to have "intimate fellowship or rapport with." Does intimate fellowship describe your present prayer relationship with the Lord? If your answer is "not really," writing out your prayers could help to establish that rapport. So often we send up ten-cent prayers expecting million-dollar answers! If we expect a return of this magnitude, we had better invest a bit more generously. As we sow, so shall we reap. If we sow little, we can expect to reap little. When we have that personal communion relationship, God becomes more real to us. He speaks to us and answers our prayers. The result is we trust Him even more and our faith in Him grows daily.

6. It Prevents Spiritual Leakage

Oswald Chambers writes:

> Spiritual leakage begins when we cease to lift up our eyes to Him. The leakage comes not so much through trouble . . . as in the imagination. It is the enemy that penetrates right into the soul and distracts the mind from God. What an enormous power there is in simple things to distract our attention from God.[2]

Having a prayer book and a place to go at the same time each day, and developing that daily discipline, frustrates the efforts of the deceiver to subtly shift our attention from the Savior.

7. It Lifts Us Out of Loneliness

Written prayer can lift us out of our loneliness, hurt, self-pity and depression and turn us around to praise, thanksgiving and rejoicing. The basic cause of negative feelings is self-focus. Writing our prayers shifts the focus from ourselves to the Lord. The result is a switch from self-pity to an attitude of praise and thanksgiving.

Many of David's psalms are beautiful examples of what can happen when we alter our focus through written prayer. Psalm 31 is a good psalm to study. Listen as David pours out his hurts:

> Pull me out of the net they have laid for me. . . . Have mercy upon me, O Lord, for I am in trouble: mine eye is consumed with grief. . . . my strength faileth. . . . my bones are consumed. . . . I am forgotten as a dead man out of mind: I am like a broken vessel. . . . They took counsel together against me. . . . they devised to take away my life!

After dumping all his hurt he turns his focus from himself to his Redeemer:

> But I trusted in thee O Lord: I said thou art my God. My times are in Thy hand. O how great is Thy goodness which Thou hast laid up for them that trust in Thee.

Then comes the praise and rejoicing:

> Blessed be the Lord: for He hath showed me His marvelous kindness. . . . O love the Lord, all ye his saints, for the Lord preserveth the faithful.

The next time pangs of pain and pity oppress you, go to your prayer book and cry out secretly to God. Continue as long as necessary until your focus turns to His goodness.

When it does, when the pain has been cleansed away, you will rejoice with David: "O clap your hands, all ye people; shout unto God with a voice of triumph!" (Psalm 47:1)

As a preparation for those difficult times, get yourself into the habit of studying Psalms. See David's true emotions being expressed and released as he turns to the Lord for strength and salvation.

8. It Puts on the "Full Armor of God"

The closer you draw yourself to the Lord, the more prone you are to the attacks and schemes of the devil. Satan never troubles himself with those who are not abiding, but he is frustrated with those he sees slipping away from his circle of influence. Ephesians 6:12 tells us "our struggle is not against flesh and blood, but against the rulers, against the powers, against the world forces of this darkness, against the spiritual forces of wickedness" (NASB).

We need protection. We need weapons. We have the helmet of salvation on at all times, but we are told to take up the shield of faith, our defensive weapon, and the sword of the Spirit (the Word of God), our offensive weapon. Notice how the Lord, when He was attacked in the wilderness by the devil, turned the Word of God upon Satan, and said in part, "'You shall not tempt the Lord your God.' . . . and the devil departed from Him until an opportune time" (Luke 4:12,13, NASB). The Lord was continually subject to attack. Are we not also?

We must put on the full armor of God daily. Is there a better way to take up our weapons for spiritual battle than to come to Him in written prayer?

9. It Strengthens Us Against Attacks

Daily prayer does not make us immune to attacks. On the contrary, we will be attacked all the more! But our daily prayer does strengthen us and keep us ready to meet those crises which can come without notice or warning. The day that starts out with beautiful sunshine may bring storm clouds in the afternoon. Tragedy, trauma and turmoil can strike at any time. We must be strengthened and prepared. Spiritual strengthening, just like physical strengthening, is a process; it takes time.

Think of an army encampment in a battle zone some two hundred years ago. The tents and supplies are pitched in the center. It is night; the troops are asleep. There are sentries posted all around to protect the perimeter. They must be alert, strong and ready. At a moment's notice they must be able to give the signal and fight any attack, any incursion or any testing for weakness by the enemy. They must be trained. They must be strong and well armed. The lives of the soldiers inside the camp depend on it.

You are the sentry who stands ready with your sword and shield. We know the enemy can never overrun the camp; he can never win. The Lord has already won the victory. But the enemy will always test us, probing for a weakness in our spiritual perimeters. Daily writing of prayers strengthens us against these inevitable attacks and crises.

10. It Allows God to Control Our Emotions

Emotions are God-given. Jesus, perfect man, God in the flesh, had emotions and displayed them. His emotions, however, never controlled Him. He was always in perfect communion with His Father in heaven. Though we can never be perfect, we can strive daily to become like Him, to have that mind and that attitude in us which was also in Christ Jesus (Philippians 2:5). As we commune with our Father in heaven, as Jesus Himself did, we allow Him to control our emotions, and gradually we shall become more and more like Him.

11. It Is the Key to Our Healing and Maturing Process

As I look back over the years I have been coming to the Lord in written prayer, there is not a shadow of doubt that it is the one significant factor that broke the block that existed in both my own spiritual and emotional growth. Even though I had been a Christian for twenty-one years, there was something missing. I did not have a deep love relationship with the Lord and my Christian life was plagued with instability. Didn't my wife and daughter see piercing, destructive anger in me? And didn't I feel hopelessly frustrated by the deep rejection that still had a secure grip on me?

It was by being obedient, by coming to the Lord in prayer, by abiding in Him, that the branch of the vine that bore little fruit is now able to bear much fruit. I have traveled well down the road on my own journey of restoration.

12. It Deepens Love and Commitment to the Lord

God formerly was a nebulous truism, real but distant and impersonal, in my life. No longer! Because I have been faithful in coming to Him, I know Him as I never knew Him before. I trust Him. I love Him with a depth of emotion that never before existed. Since I had always suppressed my painful human emotions and frustrations, I didn't even know what it meant to love Him with spiritual emotions. I now understand more completely what He did on the cross for me. I have some comprehension of the physical suffering He endured so that I might have life. Something that has helped me grasp the sacrifice Jesus made on the cross is a paper written by an unknown physician titled "The Crucifixion of Jesus." I've included it in the Additional Helps section at the end of the book. It is not easy reading, but it will help you to deepen your love and commitment to your Savior.

13. It Prevents Interference With Prayers

Do you think Satan wants you to pray? He will do everything he can to interrupt the prayers of a man or woman of God. Writing your prayers makes it that much more difficult for him to interfere.

I clearly remember one morning in September 1988. We had been back only a few days from a ministry trip to Australia. I was sitting at my desk writing my prayers. That morning I wrote about four pages. I had prayed for quite a long time and was truly blessed and in an attitude of praise and thanksgiving. I felt led then, as I do occasionally, to read over what I had just written.

Can you guess how long it took to read over about an hour's worth of written prayer? No more than four minutes! Suddenly a question popped into my mind: *Is this the best use of your time, writing out your prayer? Think of how many more people you could pray for if you prayed orally without writing!*

That message sounded so logical, so valid, and it sounded so spiritual. "Think of how many *more* people you could pray for!" Was God displeased with me writing my prayers? Was He telling me I was wasting my time and His time, too?

Instantly the answer came to me: *No. You are not wasting your time. All the time you are writing your prayers, who are you thinking about?* At once I knew the truth. In writing, my mind was stayed on the Lord, where it should be. If I stopped writing, I would be back where I was before, easily distracted and ineffective. There was no question who had asked that spiritual-sounding question. It was Satan, the prince of darkness. And the voice of the Lord was clear. It was He who gave me the answer. I thanked Him for answering both so clearly and so quickly. I have not stopped writing to Him since.

14. It Provides a Prayer Closet

The Lord specifically prescribes a prayer closet in Matthew 6:6: "But you, when you pray, enter into thy closet . . . pray to thy Father which is in secret; and thy Father which seeth in secret shall reward thee openly."

Where do you pray? Where is your prayer closet, where you can come personally and privately to the Lord? Corporate prayer, family prayer and couple's prayer are all valuable, but even the Lord retreated frequently into His own prayer closet in order to be alone with His Father. I once felt that corporate prayer was impersonal and generally unsatisfying. No one asked for prayer about deep personal issues. Then I realized that corporate church body prayer is not to be a substitute for personal prayer. The place for personal prayer is in one's own private prayer closet.

15. It Keeps Us Alert in Prayer

Few have ever fallen asleep while praying aloud in a church meeting. Few have ever dozed at the dinner table while giving thanks. It is in our private prayer closet that we need help to stay alert. Colossians 4:2 tells us: "Devote yourselves to prayer, keeping alert in it with an attitude of thanksgiving" (NASB).

Many of us don't devote ourselves to prayer because we can't keep alert in it. When our minds wander, or we doze, we are dissatisfied with ourselves, as was the Lord with Peter, James and John at Gethsemane. He asked them to "tarry ye here, and watch with me" (Matthew 26:38). Three times he returned and each time found them asleep. They were not able to stay alert and keep watch with Him! Imagine His emotional pain, knowing He would soon lay down His life for His friends, His disciples—these men who could not keep awake: "What, could ye not watch with me one hour?" (Matthew 26:40). He was willing to give His life, and they could not watch one hour.

His words ring in our minds today. Can you not keep watch with Him for one hour? Can you not devote yourself to prayer, keeping alert in it? You can when you are writing your prayers. You'll be amazed how easy it is to stay alert.

16. It Refocuses What We Want From God

Our entire childhood, it seems, was focused on getting from our parents not only what we needed but also what we wanted. As we began developing a relationship with our heavenly Father, it was only natural, therefore, that our early prayers would resemble a "want list." As spiritual babes, even though we may have been physical adults, we tended to pray as children. In Jeremiah 45:4,5, the Lord says: "Seekest thou great things for thyself? Seek them not! . . . but thy *life* will I give unto thee."

Oswald Chambers writes:

> If you have only come the length of asking God for things, you have never come to the first strand of abandonment. "I did ask God for the Holy Spirit, but He did not give me the rest and the peace I expected." God puts His finger on the reason—you are not seeking the Lord at all, you are seeking something for yourself. When you draw near to God, you cease asking for things . . . "Your Father knoweth what *things* ye have need of, before ye ask Him" . . . Then why ask? That you may get to know Him. God wants you in a closer relationship to Himself than receiving His gifts; He wants you to get to *know Him.*
>
> He is not concerned about making you blessed and happy just now; He is working out His ultimate perfection all the time . . . "that they may be one even as We are" . . . When you abandon to God, you will be the most delighted creature on earth; God has got you absolutely and has given you your life.[3]

What is it that you want from God? Is it in line with what God wants for you? Your daily written focus on the

Lord will enable you to agree with Paul, "I count all things to be loss in view of the surpassing value of *knowing Christ Jesus* my Lord . . . that I may know Him, and the power of His resurrection and the fellowship of His sufferings, being conformed to His death" (Philippians 3:8,10, NASB).

Other Benefits of Written Prayer

17. *It Is a Written Record* of what God has taught, what I have learned and where I have been.

18. *There Are Rich Re-blessings* in going back and reading past prayers.

19. *It Unleashes a Stream of Prayer Concerns.* Previously I had to think of people or things to pray for. Now they come over me like a flood.

20. *It Becomes a Bearing of Burdens* for others instead of simply "praying for others." Through written prayer the Lord revealed to me what it means to be a Simon of Cyrene, the man chosen to bear the Lord's burden.

21. *It Allows for Scriptural Confirmation of God's Responses* at a later time. One that I remember vividly happened some time ago. I was talking to the Lord about my perception that Florence was not meeting my emotional needs. He told me I was not to emphasize telling her "I love you" so that she would tell me back, but I was to *show* her how much I love her.

About two weeks later I was studying through 1 John. I came across a verse that I had seen many times before: "Little children, let us not love with word or with tongue, but in deed and truth" (1 John 3:18, NASB). I had seen that before, but I had never *seen* it as He revealed it to me at that moment! I was in awe of the wondrous power of the Lord, for I remembered clearly what He told me two weeks previously. In my Bible I immediately paraphrased, "Love is not an explanation, not a proclamation. Love is a demonstration."

22. *It Lifts Prayer to a Higher Plane.* I have known joy, praise, thanksgiving, spiritual emotion and ecstasy in prayer such as I never before knew could be possible.

23. *It Is the Working Out of What God Has Worked In.* Listening to a lecture on refereeing basketball does not make me a referee, any more than watching a Stormie Omartian exercise video strengthens my muscles. I have to get in there and do it myself.

24. *It Is a Deliberate Act of Worship.* The whole concept of worship has taken on new meaning as my written prayer life develops. I worship the Lord daily. Invariably I begin my communion with Him in praise and thanksgiving, gradually drifting into other areas and returning at the conclusion to fervent expressions of love and adoration. When I sit down with prayer book in hand, I come specifically to worship Him, to exalt His name.

This discussion certainly does not cover all the benefits of written prayer, for the blessings and thoughts of the Lord are more in number than the sands by the sea. It is but for us to tap into that well from which springs the river of living waters.

Part IV

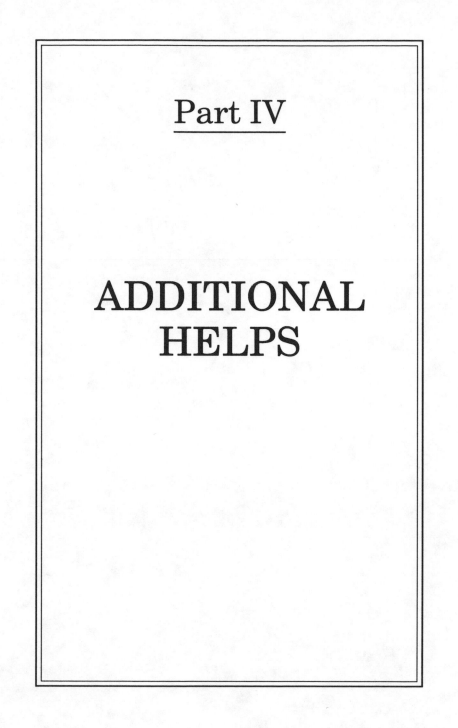

ADDITIONAL HELPS

18

SOME SECRETS OF EFFECTIVE PRAYER

Prayer is the foundation of our whole Christian life. It is the way we come to our Father in heaven, to talk, to share, to commune. It is how we fulfill our Lord's instruction to abide in Him. When we pray we obey Him. When we pray we are following His example, for Jesus Himself communed regularly with His Father in heaven.

Prayer is the means of tapping into the power that is available to us. It is the method God has given us to know Him, grow in Him and develop our trust relationship.

Despite all of this, personal prayer is usually the most neglected aspect of our spiritual life. We are too busy, active or occupied to set aside time for prayer.

I remember reading a biography of Martin Luther, in which he was quoted as saying, "I have so much to do today, I could never get through it all. So I think I will spend the first three hours in prayer." At the time, I wondered how he could spend three hours in prayer. Now I understand!

We tend to relegate the discipline of prayer to either the moments when we have time (which never seems to happen), or when we are in a crisis.

Changing Your Prayer Habit

Writing our prayers is nothing more than writing down what we would otherwise speak orally or think silently. We can also think of it as writing a daily letter to our Father in heaven. It is no more complicated than that.

There are no rights or wrongs. The only "wrong" you could commit is not doing it.

Writing my prayers is the most effective way I know of going into my prayer closet to be alone and quiet with the Lord. Since the Lord generally speaks to me in a still, small voice, I allow myself to be in the position and the condition to hear His voice: writing silently with my mind focused on Him. If I were rushing around sending up "arrow prayers," it is unlikely I would ever hear His voice.

How do I know when I hear His voice? Is it audible? No. But there have been occasions when it was so clear, it could have been audible. I know that it is His voice when I am writing my prayer and a distinct godly thought comes to me. Other times, a certain Bible verse or truth comes to my mind which specifically relates to something I am talking to my Father about. I get excited when I realize the Lord has revealed His truth to me. At other times, a certain name will suddenly come to mind for whom I should intercede. Writing my prayers is a deliberate step of putting myself in a position to hear His voice.

In Luke 18:1, we read, "Then he spoke a parable to them, that men always ought to pray and not lose heart." The Lord uses a parable to show us not only that we should pray, but that we should come continually to the Father. He likes to hear from us!

To Whom Should We Pray?

To whom should we pray? There are many names for God in the Scriptures. He is God. He is Jehovah. He is our heavenly Father. He is the Lord Jesus Christ. Dick Purnell has written an excellent little study titled *Knowing God By His Names* (Here's Life Publishers) which helps readers understand and appreciate who God is, what He does for us, and the depths of His love for us. Addressing God by His various names brings honor to Him and, at the same time, enriches your personal understanding and appreciation of Him.

Some people who were victimized by their earthly fathers may have trouble addressing God as "Father." If this is your situation, you may find it helpful to address Him by His other names until your journey of restoration has brought you to a point where you can comprehend the infinite difference between your earthly father (a human being full of sin, lust, pride and other weaknesses) and your heavenly Father, the God of the universe who loves you so much that He gave His only Son to die for you.

Jean, who experienced several forms of childhood abuse at the hands of her father, told us that she struggled with the concept of a loving "heavenly Father" until she did a study of 1 Corinthians 13. Since God is love, she reasoned, then the "love chapter" of God's Word describes (1) what God is not, and (2) what He is—in His personal relationship with her. "I actually drew a line down a sheet of notebook paper and headed the left column *What God Is Not* and the right column *What God Is*," Jean says. "After I completed both lists from 1 Corinthians 13, I realized for the first time how utterly different my heavenly Father is from my earthly father—and I could now address Him as 'Father.'"

Keep Journal and Prayer Notebook Separate

It's important to note that written prayer is *not* journaling. Many people who are seeking and searching for truth are in the practice of periodically writing down feelings, emotions and experiences. Journaling is a healthy and helpful exercise that enables you to keep track of various thoughts that flash into your mind.

If you journal, we strongly suggest that you use a separate book for your written prayers to enable you to keep your prayer life distinct from your journal. Those who have begun by using one book for both purposes often find they start out in prayer, but soon drift off into journaling. Journaling is helpful, but praying is *essential.*

Parts of Prayer

As you think about what you want to say to your Father in prayer, a good guide word is *FACTS*.

F	**F**AITH: the foundation of all prayer
A	**A**DORATION: your expression of love to the Lord
C	**C**ONFESSION: your admission or agreement with the Lord
T	**T**HANKSGIVING: your expression of praise and appreciation for who *He is* more than for what *He has done* for you
S	**S**UPPLICATION: your requests that you bring to the Lord for yourself and others.

FACTS is a good formula for your prayer. Each part does not necessarily have to be present each time you pray, but it will help you on those days when you feel your stream of prayers might be "drying up."

The Psalms also provide excellent guidelines for our prayers. In Psalm 31:3, for example, we pick up two ideas that are perfectly appropriate for prayer.

> Thou art my rock and my fortress; therefore for Thy name's sake *lead me,* and *guide me.*

As you face decisions or clouds of uncertainty, ask Him to lead and guide you. You might want to begin your prayer by writing out this verse and then telling the Lord how this verse applies to your needs today, making it a part of your prayer. Use psalms as models for your own prayers.

Another valuable example of a guideline prayer is made by the Syrophoenician woman in Matthew 15:25. She came "and worshipped him, saying, 'Lord, help me.'" It is no doubt the shortest prayer in the Bible. But the Lord has always immediately answered when I have asked Him to help me by showing me *my* part of the problem. The problem is, I have not always remembered to ask Him to show me! The woman in this passage had a serious problem: She couldn't stand to live with her daughter. She came to the Lord asking for mercy and pity because of her daughter, and left acknowledging there were problems in her own life that needed to be addressed. When she prayed, "Lord, help me," and was willing to admit her part of the problem, "her daughter was made whole from that very hour" (Matthew 15:28).

Pray for Others

A final important part of prayer is intercessory prayer. In the words of Oswald Chambers, "Intercession means we rouse ourselves up to get the mind of Christ about the one for whom we pray."[1] Our prayer for others focuses on knowing Christ's purpose for them. This may prove to be vastly different from our plans for them! Listen to the words of our Lord:

> I do not ask in behalf of these alone, but for those also who believe in Me through their word; that they may all be one, even as Thou, Father, art in me, and I in thee . . . that they may be one, just as we are one (John 17:20-22, NASB).

Not only is He our intercessor, but He also teaches us to be intercessors.

For a rewarding time of Bible study, look carefully at some of our Lord's prayers as recorded in Matthew 11:25, Matthew 26:39, Luke 3:21, Luke 6:12, Luke 9:29, Luke 23:34, John 6:15, and John 17.

When to Pray

If you are going to be successful in developing a disciplined written prayer life, you will need to set aside a certain time of the day as *the time* you reserve for the Lord. Most people find that first thing in the morning suits them the best. This seems to be confirmed by Matthew 6:33: "Seek ye *first* the kingdom of God and His righteousness." In the early morning we are alert and fresh. Our minds have not yet been distracted by the events of the day. A young mother with little children who demand her attention first thing in the morning, or a husband who has to be on the job at 6 A.M., may find it impossible to set aside time early in the morning. That's okay. Each one of us has been given twenty-four hours in each day. Our task is to find one of those twenty-four hours to spend with Him.

Suppose, as a victim of childhood interference, you were to go to a spiritual doctor to have your emotional cancer treated. His prescription for guaranteed health was 180 doses of a powerful yet inexpensive pill. You have a decision to make, don't you? You can choose to follow his advice, or you can choose to ignore it.

If you choose to follow his advice, you will then have to decide, "How often should I take these pills? I'm very busy. I have a family to take care of and a job that requires quite a bit of time. I don't think I could take more than one pill a week."

According to that schedule, it would take three-and-a-half years to cure your emotional cancer. When you tell your doctor your plan, he would undoubtedly reply, "No, that will never work. They are not nearly as effective if you only take them once a week. You have to take one each and every day. If you do, you will feel significant improvement in just a short time. Eventually, you will see such great changes you will want to keep taking these pills for the rest of your life. They will also protect you from any possible future attacks of your cancer."

Do you know the name of your doctor? He is the Great Physician. His name is the Lord Jesus Christ. His pill is prayer, the daily coming to Him, submitting to Him, learning from Him. He will "give you rest for your weary soul."

How long should you pray? Read the Gethsemane story again in Matthew 26. Following the Last Supper, Jesus went "with them unto a place called Gethsemane, and saith unto the disciples, 'Sit ye here, while I go and pray.'" He took with Him Peter, James and John, and admitted to them, "My soul is exceedingly sorrowful even unto death, tarry ye here and watch with me."

After going a little farther, Jesus fell on His face and cried out in prayer to His Father, "O my Father, if it be possible, let this cup [His upcoming death on the cross] pass from me: nevertheless not as I will, but as thou wilt." Imagine the pain He felt as He returned to His disciples only to find that they had fallen asleep! Hear the deep hurt in His voice as He awakens them, "Could ye not keep watch with me for one hour?"

There is no magic in praying for one hour. Clearly the Lord asked Peter, James and John to keep watch with Him for one hour. I personally believe He is asking that of us today as well. If we are serious about wanting to abide in Him, to become like Him, to receive His healing, we will desire to give Him one hour each day. If we give Him less, we show Him we regard Him less.

How often should we come to Him? The Scriptures give us the answer. To refer to but a few:

Psalm 61:8	I will sing praise unto thy name forever, that I may *daily* perform my vows.
Psalm 72:15	Prayer also shall be made for him continually and *daily* shall he be praised.

Psalm 88:9	Lord, I have called *daily* upon thee, I have stretched out my hands unto thee.
Psalm 145:2	*Every day* will I bless thee; and I will praise thy name forever and ever.
Luke 9:23	If any man will come after me, let him deny himself, take up his cross *daily* and follow me.

Writing our prayers daily comes into clear alignment with these verses. Coming before God daily helps us to deny ourselves and our personal goals, lift Him up into our lives, and follow Him.

Are you ready now to set aside one hour of each day to be with the Lord? You will be tapping into a reservoir of spiritual riches whose depths will take a lifetime to discover. Don't let one more day pass without beginning this rewarding spiritual discipline.

19

PRAYER STARTERS

Often I begin my written prayer with the word of the Lord as recorded in Matthew 11:25: "I praise Thee, O Father, Lord of heaven and earth that Thou . . . " and then I continue with whatever is on my heart that day. Sometimes I come to my prayer closet with needs or thoughts on my mind. Other days I have no agenda. I just start to write. Many times a verse in the Scriptures will set off my prayers.

Our recommendation to you is to start off each day by studying Oswald Chambers' thought for the day in *My Utmost for His Highest.* You will want to underline or highlight specific concepts or sentences that are significant to you. Highlighting key phrases will enable you to mine the wealth of wisdom in this outstanding book.

Following your reading in Chambers, pursue a plan of study in the Scriptures. Many types have already been suggested. We strongly recommend using the *Thompson Chain Reference Bible.* It has a wealth of additional information and resources. It is available in the *King James* or *New International* version. For my personal study, I am partial to the *New American Standard Bible.* It also contains excellent chain references, especially in the New Testament.

Having completed your study of the Scriptures, it is time to take up your pen and begin your deliberate act of worship. To assist you in beginning your own book of prayer, I have put together a list of thirty-six prayer-starter verses. Simply write out the suggested verse and then continue the thoughts expressed in the verse in your own words. For example, using Psalm 9:1,2 for a starter, you'd write: "I will praise thee, O Lord, with all my whole heart. I will be glad and rejoice in thee: I will sing praises to thy name" and then continue writing in your own words.

Here's how one might continue the above thought:

> Lord Jesus, I thank you today for the joy of coming to You in prayer. I can't believe that You are here, hearing every beat of my heart, but I know You are. I will praise You today with my lips and my heart. You have chosen me to be Your own; I am loved. Lord, help me to love others today the way You love me . . .

Whenever you feel a little dry and need something to prime your pump, try one of these prayer starters:

Day

1. "I will praise thee, O Lord, with all my whole heart. I will be glad and rejoice in thee: I will sing praises to thy name" (Psalm 9:1,2).
2. "Peace I leave with you; My peace I give to you; not as the world gives, do I give to you. Let not your heart be troubled, nor let it be fearful" (John 14:27, NASB).
3. "Thou will keep him in perfect peace whose mind is stayed on Thee: because he trusteth in Thee" (Isaiah 26:3).
4. "Since He Himself was tempted in that which He has suffered, He is able to come to the aid of those who are tempted" (Hebrews 2:18, NASB).
5. "Keep watching and praying, that you may not enter into temptation; the spirit is willing, but the flesh is weak" (Matthew 26:41, NASB).
6. "I have prayed for you that your faith may not fail" (Luke 22:32, NASB).

7. "God of all comfort; who comforts us in all our affliction, so that we may be able to comfort those who are in any affliction" (2 Corinthians 1:3,4, NASB).
8. "Seek ye first the kingdom of God, and His righteousness, and all these things shall be added unto you" (Matthew 6:33).
9. "He who abides in Me, and I in him, he bears much fruit; for apart from Me you can do nothing" (John 15:5, NASB).
10. "She came and began to bow down before Him, saying, 'Lord, help me'" (Matthew 15:25, NASB).
11. "Save me, O God, for the waters are come in unto my soul. I sink in deep mire, where there is no standing: I am come into deep waters where the floods overflow me. I am weary of my crying; my throat is dried: mine eyes fail while I wait for my God" (Psalm 69:1-3).
12. "Could ye not keep watch with Me for one hour?" (Matthew 26:40)
13. "This kind cannot come out by anything but prayer" (Mark 9:29, NASB).
14. "Although he was a son, He learned obedience from the things which He suffered" (Hebrews 5:8, NASB).
15. "I praise Thee, O Father, Lord of heaven and earth" (Luke 10:21, NASB).
16. "Whatever is true, whatever is honorable, whatever is right, whatever is pure, whatever is lovely, whatever is of good repute, if there is any excellence and if anything worthy of praise, let your mind dwell on these things" (Philippians 4:8, NASB).

17. "Always giving thanks for all things in the name of our Lord Jesus Christ" (Ephesians 5:20, NASB).
18. "And the Lord turned the captivity of Job, when he prayed for his friends" (Job 42:10).
19. "You, too, now have sorrow, but I will see you again, and your heart will rejoice, and no one takes your joy away from you" (John 16:22, NASB).
20. "I do not ask in behalf of these alone, but for those also who believe in me" (John 17:20).
21. "Truly, truly, I say to you, that you will weep and lament . . . but your sorrow will be turned to joy" (John 16:20, NASB).
22. "We do not lose heart . . . our inner man is being renewed day by day" (2 Corinthians 4:16, NASB).
23. "Not one of us lives for himself . . . we live for the Lord . . . whether we live or die; we are the Lord's" (Romans 14:7,8, NASB).
24. "We who are strong ought to bear the weaknesses of those without strength, and not just please ourselves . . . for even Christ did not please Himself" (Romans 15:1,3, NASB).
25. "You shall love the Lord your God with all your heart, with all your soul, and with all your mind" (Matthew 22:37, NASB).
26. "For we are His workmanship, created in Christ Jesus for good works, which God prepared beforehand, that we should walk in them" (Ephesians 2:10, NASB).
27. "He rejoiced greatly in the Holy Spirit, and said, 'I praise Thee, O Father, Lord of heaven and earth'" (Luke 10:21, NASB).

28. "Enter into His gates with thanksgiving, and into His courts with praise, be thankful unto Him, and bless His name" (Psalm 100:4).

29. "I count all things to be loss in view of the surpassing value of knowing Christ Jesus my Lord" (Philippians 3:8, NASB).

30. "Come to Me all who are weary and heavy laden, and I will give you rest. Take My yoke upon you, and learn from Me . . . and you shall find rest for your souls" (Matthew 11:28,29, NASB).

31. "Now that you know this truth, how happy you will be if you put it into practice" (John 13:17, TEV).

32. "Without faith it is impossible to please Him, for He that cometh to God must believe that He is and that He is a rewarder of them that diligently seek Him" (Hebrews 11:6).

33. "O God, thou knowest my foolishness; and my sins are not hid from Thee" (Psalm 69:5).

34. "My prayer is unto Thee, O Lord, in an acceptable time. O God, in the multitude of Thy mercy hear me" (Psalm 69:13).

35. "I will praise the name of God with a song, and will magnify Him with thanksgiving. O Lord, our Lord, how excellent is Thy name in all the earth!" (Psalm 69:30; 8:9)

36. "This is the day which the Lord hath made; we will rejoice and be glad in it" (Psalm 118:24).

20

"FORGIVE? HOW CAN I?"

Probably the most difficult question a victim will ask is "How can I possibly forgive the person who did this to me?"

The answer is, you can't. You alone do not have the ability to forgive the person who victimized you. And that is not a sin. That is not something for which you should feel ashamed or guilty.

There is one, though, who can enable you to do what you cannot do yourself. He has the power to give you the ability to forgive. You will be able to forgive out of a heart that is filled with your love for the one who has already demonstrated His love for you by His death on the cross.

Perhaps the greatest demonstration of supernatural forgiveness in all of history is when Jesus prayed to His Father as He hung on the cross, "Forgive them; for they know not what they do" (Luke 23:34).

He now reigns eternally to enable us to do what we may not be able to do on our own—forgive those who have committed sins against us just as He forgave those who sinned against Him.

Forgiving When It's Hardest

There are two other inspiring illustrations of forgiveness in Scripture.

The first is Joseph, whose saga of being sold into slavery by his malicious older brothers is told in Genesis.

As a result of the sins committed against him, Joseph suffered intense affliction and deprivation. But God blessed Joseph for his faithfulness and steadfastness, and used him to redeem his entire family from famine in Israel (see Genesis 42—45).

Joseph's moving words of forgiveness are recorded in Genesis 45:4,5,7:

> Joseph said unto his brethren, "Come near to me, I pray you. . . . I am Joseph your brother, whom ye sold into Egypt. Now therefore be not grieved, nor angry with yourselves . . . God did send me before you to preserve life, to preserve you . . . and to save your lives by a great deliverance."

From a human standpoint it seems impossible that Joseph not only forgave his brothers, but also preserved and delivered. Only with the power of God is someone able to forgive as Joseph did. And this same power is available to you. You can come to Him for that power to forgive. He makes it available to you.

The second beautiful and equally incomprehensible illustration of forgiveness is found in Acts 6—7. Stephen is described as a man full of faith and the Holy Spirit. He and six others were chosen to fulfill administration responsibilities to enable the disciples to devote themselves to prayer and the ministry of the gospel. In addition to these duties, Stephen was soon speaking out with wisdom and power. Many of the Jewish leaders felt threatened and had him arrested and tried before the Council. Acts 7 describes his testimony of defense. His words were so convicting that the Jewish leaders were angered all the more. They ran upon him in their rage, cast him out of the city and stoned him to death:

> Stephen, calling upon God, and saying, "Lord Jesus, receive my spirit" . . . kneeled down, and cried with a loud voice, "Lord, lay not this sin to their charge" (Acts 7:59,60).

His last words spoke of forgiveness for those who attacked him. He had seen the glory of the Lord and was able to ask the unthinkable. It was the Lord who enabled Stephen to ask that this sin not be laid to their charge.

Christ's example and His power enable you to forgive, no matter the circumstances. Jesus promises: "Behold, I give you power . . . over all the power of the enemy" (Luke 10:19).

Choosing to Forgive

Forgiveness is a choice. You control the process. No one forces you to forgive, and the person being forgiven needn't cooperate. Forgiveness relies solely on the forgiver. You can decide to do nothing and remain in misery, or you can decide to forgive. The acid of anger eats away only at the container.

Patty McConnell, in *A Workbook for Healing,* writes:

> [Sometimes we feel that we] can't forgive because of the depth of a wound or its newness. That's normal. But not to forgive grafts you to the past like a flowering branch to a disfigured tree. Others won't forgive out of pride or the need for revenge. But do you want to get even or get well? Pride and revenge halt the healing; they boomerang to deepen the wound by reaffirming the old tapes that say you are bad or unlovable.[1]

Revenge or retribution is not your responsibility; it is the Lord's:

> For it is written, "Vengeance is mine, I will repay," says the Lord (Romans 12:19, NASB).
>
> The Lord shall fight for you, and ye shall hold your peace (Exodus 14:14, NASB).

Dr. Gerald Jampolsky, author of *Love Is Letting Go of Fear,* makes this comment:

> The unforgiving mind . . . is certain of the justification of its anger and the correctness of its condemning judgment. The unforgiving mind rigidly sees the past and future as the same and is resistant to change, sees itself as innocent, and others as guilty. It thrives on conflict and on being right. It perceives everything as separate.[2]

You must take the initiative to forgive. The Lord will give you the enabling grace when you are willing.

The Command to Forgive

We cannot escape the fact that forgiveness is a command. In another significant "If we . . . then He" verse, our Lord says:

> If you forgive men for their transgressions, your heavenly Father will also forgive you. But if you do not forgive men, then your Father will not forgive your transgressions. . . . Should you not also have had mercy on your fellow slave, even as I had mercy on you? (Matthew 6:14,15; 18:33, NASB).

In Colossians 3:12,13 we are further directed:

> And so, as thou who have been chosen of God, holy and beloved, put on a heart of compassion, kindness, . . . bearing with one another, and forgiving each other, whoever has a complaint against anyone; just as the Lord forgave you, so also should you (NASB).

The Lord then, both by His example and by His enabling, prepares the way for us to make the choice. But this choice is, in fact, no choice at all for those of us who belong to Him. We must obey His command. We must obey if we wish to abide and be restored.

Putting the Truths Into Practice

Knowing these truths is just the beginning. You have to put them into practice. Here are eight principles and steps you can follow to aid the work of the Lord's forgiveness in your heart. To cement each point in your mind, write the verses in the space provided.[3]

1. Forgiveness is an act of the will. You have to want to forgive. Philippians 2:13 (TEV or Good News version):

____

____

2. You will not be forgiven by God unless you forgive others who have hurt you. Mark 11:25,26:

____

____

3. Think of all that God has forgiven you. Ephesians 4:32:

____

____

List below several things which you know God has already forgiven you.

1.________________	5.________________
2.________________	6.________________
3.________________	7.________________
4.________________	8.________________

4. Thank the Lord for any blessings you have received from those who have hurt you. Ephesians 4:20:

____

____

5. Think of the needs of those who hurt you. Their needs and their pain may be as great as yours. Galatians 6:2:

____

____

6. Ask God to give you His supernatural ability to forgive them through His love for you. Luke 23:34a:

____

____

7. Ask God to give you opportunities to express His love to them through you, both in word and in deed. 1 John 3:17,18:

____

____

8. If the one who hurt you is living, begin regularly praying for that person. If not, think of and pray for another person who has hurt you. Matthew 5:44,45:

____

____

Corrie Ten Boom, author of *The Hiding Place,* struggled with forgiving a man whom it would seem deserved no forgiveness. She had been speaking in a church in Germany, and following the service a man walked up to talk with her. In an instant she recognized him. Her mind flashed back to the concentration camp where she and her sister Betsie had been imprisoned, and where Betsie had died from the persecution. That man had been one of the Nazi S.S. guards.

And suddenly it was all there—the roomful of mocking men, the heaps of clothing, Betsie's pain-blanched face.

He came up to me as the church was emptying, beaming and bowing. "How grateful I am for your message, *Fraulein,*" he said. "To think that, as you say, He has washed my sins away!"

His hand was thrust out to shake mine. And I, who had preached so often . . . the need to forgive, kept my hand at my side.

Even as the angry, vengeful thoughts boiled through me, I saw the sin of them. Jesus Christ had died for this man; was I going to ask for more? *Lord Jesus,* I prayed, *forgive me and help me to forgive him.*

I tried to smile. I struggled to raise my hand. I could not. I felt nothing, not the slightest spark of warmth or charity. And so again I breathed a silent prayer. *Jesus, I cannot forgive him. Give me Your forgiveness.*

As I took his hand, the most incredible thing happened. From my shoulder along my arm and through my hand a current seemed to pass from me to him, while into my heart sprang a love for this stranger that almost overwhelmed me.

And so I discovered that it is not on our forgiveness any more than on our goodness that the world's healing hinges, but on His. When He tells us to love our enemies, He gives along with the command, the love itself.[4]

Forgiveness is a crucial step in the journey of restoration. As He made it possible for Corrie Ten Boom, and for countless others as well, He will make it possible for you, if you are willing and if you obey. He can make forgiveness a reality.

21

THE PRAYER OFFERED IN FAITH

The promise of restoration is a journey. Healing may not come easily. There may be deep valleys ahead, through which we must walk.

You will be tempted to give up. You may be following the steps to healing faithfully and still not feel any better about yourself or any closer to the Lord. You may think, *This isn't working. There must be a better way.* When such thoughts come to mind, you can be sure who is placing them there. It is the enemy who has kept you in bondage for so many years. He does not want you to be set free. Make no mistake: Our struggle is not against flesh and blood but against the powers and rulers of darkness.

During times of discouragement at the slow rate of progress, we need to remind ourselves of Paul's words: "We also exult [rejoice] in our tribulations; knowing that tribulation brings about perseverance; and perseverance, proven character; and proven character, hope" (Romans 5:3,4, NASB). During times of discouragement, let us persevere. Let us continue walking down that road of our journey, ever yoked with Him who alone has the power to heal, teach and strengthen us.

During those days of discouragement, let us remember to be thankful: "*Always* giving thanks for *all things* in the name of our Lord Jesus Christ to God even the Father" (Ephesians 5:20, NASB). He will give us hope as He daily works in us to conform us to His image.

Rejoicing, giving thanks and persevering serve to build our faith. The promise of healing is based on faith—our faith in the person of the Lord Jesus Christ: "And without faith it is impossible to please Him, for he who comes to God must believe that He is, and that He is a rewarder of those who seek Him" (Hebrews 11:6, NASB).

Many have been healed because of their faith:

> The blind men came up to Him, and Jesus said to them, "Do you believe that I am able to do this?" They said to Him, "Yes, Lord." Then He touched their eyes, saying, "Be it done to you according to your faith" (Matthew 10:28,29).
>
> "O woman, great is thy faith: be it unto thee even as thou wilt." And her daughter was made whole from that very hour (Matthew 15:28).
>
> And he said to the woman, "Thy faith hath saved thee, go in peace" (Luke 7:50).
>
> And he said unto him, "Arise, go thy way: thy faith hath made thee whole" (Luke 17:19).
>
> And Jesus . . . asked him . . . "What wilt thou that I shall do unto thee?" And he said, "Lord, that I may receive my sight." And Jesus said unto him, "Receive thy sight: thy faith hath saved thee" (Luke 18:40-42).

As you continually and daily come to Him in prayer, He will build your faith. You will develop a trust relationship deeper than you have ever known before. You will learn the joy of an intimate communion with the living, loving God.

As your journey continues, you will look back, from time to time, and see how far you have come. One day you'll notice that the old feelings of rejection just aren't triggered anymore. The pains of interference are gradually disappearing. You may not know exactly when or how, but you will know that you are different. He has been working His transforming work in your life, your emotions and your relationships.

And as long as you continue coming to Him, you can be "confident of this very thing, that He who began a good work in you will perfect it until the day of Christ Jesus" (Philippians 1:6, NASB).

Then you will be able to rejoice with David:

> The Lord hath heard my supplication; the Lord will receive my prayer (Psalm 6:9).
>
> O Lord my God, I cried unto thee, and thou hast healed me (Psalm 30:2).
>
> I will bless the Lord at all times: His praise shall continually be in my mouth (Psalm 34:1).
>
> I will praise thee, O Lord, among the people: I will sing unto thee among the nations (Psalm 57:9).
>
> O clap your hands, all ye people; shout unto God with the voice of triumph (Psalm 47:1).

Appendix A

ANSWERS TO SOME OF YOUR QUESTIONS

What is the difference between counseling, therapy and healing?

Counseling is giving good, helpful advice. It provides solutions for known problems to people who are able to implement them. Counseling is giving good, helpful advice. Counseling is the exercising of wisdom.

Therapy is a method of figuring out what damage has been done to one's minds or emotions. Therapy is useful when the origin of the problem is unknown. When apparently good counsel is ineffective, therapy is recommended. Therapy should be considered whenever attempts to correct problems end repeatedly in helplessness, frustration, confusion or passivity.

Healing is the removal of pain or damage left by an injury. Our souls, bodies and spirits can be injured. Healing can only remove the pain and destructiveness of the wound, though, not the scar. Every time our souls are injured they need healing.

The best guideline for seeking help, whether counseling, therapy or healing, is your own feelings. When you feel you need help, seek it.

Do I have to go to a counselor?

You ought to go to a counselor when the turmoil in your life is so unbearable that you don't think you can handle it any longer; when you feel suicidal; when your mind is so muddled you can't function normally; when you have questions that seem to have no answers; when you are not making any progress in your healing journey; when you feel you need help; when you need the wisdom of someone with knowledge and experience. Usually, you do not need to go to a professional counselor just to have someone to talk to.

How can I find a good counselor?

Recommendations are most important. Ask your pastor or a friend who has found someone in whom he or she has confidence. If you have to select someone from the Yellow Pages, do not hesitate to ask about that person's qualifications and experience with victims of interference. If he resents your questions, it will probably be better to find someone else.

Must my counselor be a Christian?

We strongly recommend you try to find a counselor who is not only a Christian, but who also counsels from a biblical perspective. Some counselors who say they are Christians work from a purely psychological perspective without ever helping the victim draw upon the healing power of Christ.

Non-Christian counselors with wisdom and compassion can be very helpful, but beware of any counselor who belittles or tries to dissuade you from your faith.

Do not be afraid to change counselors if you feel you are receiving questionable counsel. Any counselor who tries to control you or won't answer your questions should be avoided.

A counselor becomes a confidante and being able to have trust and a comfortable relationship is very important.

Further helpful guidance can be found in our book, "Get a Life, Without the Strife" (Nashville: Thomas Nelson, Inc., 1993).

Is it necessary to confront the victimizer?

This is a question that has no easy answer. The decision to confront should be made only after confirmation from the Lord through prayer—never impulsively and never until significant healing has taken place in your own life. Florence and I personally feel that, in most cases, confrontation raises more problems than it solves. It should not be undertaken without the benefit of both wise counsel and the reading of as much resource material as possible.

Often the benefits of confrontation can be achieved by writing a letter to the offender and never sending it. You are able to express your feelings on paper and that may provide the release you need. There may be no further advantage to mailing the letter. In fact, mailing such a letter often causes new problems rather than resolving the old.

Bear in mind that it is rare for a confronted offender to admit, confess and repent. In most cases, the result is anger, denial or casting the blame back on you. Once again, caution with confrontation.

What about forgetting the past?

There is no reason to look for a snake under every rock. We do not recommend looking for trouble where there is none. If well enough is well enough, then leave well enough alone.

But if there are problems, issues or hurts that persist and resist all efforts to heal, we need to examine our past for possible roots. When there is garbage in our life, we must take it to the curb to be taken away. Philippians 3:13 is often used out of context and must be taken in light of the whole passage in this regard. Paul says that he, too, suffered many things and made many mistakes. But he is not going to wait until he is perfect, nor will he allow himself to dwell upon or be consumed by the past. He will press on for what lies ahead. This may be called "Service While in the Process."

Do I need to remember every instance of abuse in my childhood?

What is important is to know what happened and who was involved. For some victims, the recovery of just one memory is completely sufficient. For others, there is a need to uncover more if they occurred. The individual with multiple victimizations will probably not find it necessary, or even wise, to try to recover every one. Let the Spirit of God guide you. He will if you ask.

Where can I get help if there are no counselors available in my area? Where can I get information on "Promise of Healing" conferences or other resources to help me in my recovery?

Our office in California is available to guide you to resources or help for recovery. You may call (619) 471-0233 for information.

Appendix B

SUMMARY OF GENERAL PRINCIPLES RELATING TO VICTIMS OF CHILDHOOD SEXUAL INTERFERENCE

1. An emotionally healthy person is rarely attracted to an emotionally unhealthy person.
2. Our emotions remember what our mind has forgotten.
3. Awareness of interference is the first step to freedom.
4. Interference is significantly more prevalent in families with strict attitudes against family nudity.
5. Absence of memory does not indicate absence of violation.
6. Sexual interference distorts and disrupts the normal and natural sexual development of a boy or girl.
7. Sexual interference destroys or weakens a child's natural defenses against later inappropriate sexual contact.
8. Sexual interference is the result, not the cause, of a breakdown in a family.
9. A child is not created by God with prevailing feelings of anger, rejection, hate or depression.
10. Gaps in childhood memory are a significant indication that a child's body and emotions were probably defiled by sexual trauma.

11. Eyes are the mirror of the soul. Sparkle reflects joy and serenity reflects inner peace. Sexual trauma is frequently reflected by pain, deadness, fear or intensity.

12. Release from inner turmoil comes with recognition, and restoration comes with the Redeemer.

13. Jesus Christ is faithful and just to cleanse us from the sins that were committed against us (1 John 1:9).

14. Virtually all victims of childhood sexual interference have low self-esteem. They feel dirty, unwanted, used or unlovable.

15. Unexplained feelings of hatred, anger, fear or stress are an almost certain symptom of sexual interference.

16. Intellectual assent to forgiveness is often ineffective when the victim does not know what or why she is forgiving.

17. When several siblings show symptoms or instability, the interference will tend to be found within the family structure.

18. People tend to marry on similar levels of pain, even when the trauma is unknown. Victims usually marry victims.

19. The dogmatically protective parent and the reactionary spouse may be hiding their own perversions, guilt or childhood trauma.

20. The energy required to maintain suppression of traumatic pain drains the individual, often resulting in passivity, depression and defeat (see Psalm 32:46, NIV).

21. The spouse of a victim becomes the secondary victim and may take on symptoms such as guilt and anger transmitted by the emotions of the victim.

22. "Deliverance" experiences that do not deal with the repressed trauma are apt to amplify the shame, guilt, discouragement and resignation when the victim finds the symptoms recurring.
23. Victims are often not content at doing what they are good at and are apt to blunder in areas in which they are not qualified.
24. Satan is always on the prowl, ready to reopen the healed-over areas of hurt and pain.
25. The victim personality accepts abuse as a normal way of life.
26. The victim personality is often unable to see the truth about himself.
27. Adult uncontrollable anger is usually the result of the sins and hurts that were committed against the child.

Appendix C

POSSIBLE ADULT SYMPTOMS OF CHILDHOOD SEXUAL INTERFERENCE

Abortion
Absence of grief at death
Abused father
Abused mother
Abusive opposite-sex
Affairs during marriage
Age forty trauma
Agoraphobia
Alcoholism—parents
Alcoholism—self
Allergy hypersensitivity
Amenorrhea/late menses
Anger
Anorexia
Anxiety
Asthma
Bad dreams
Bad feelings about Masonic Temple
Bad rooms/houses
BiPolar disease
Body has no value
Candles in dreams
Chased in dreams
Childhood depression
Childhood fear—something under bed
Childhood masturbation
Childhood teeth grinding
Childhood view of adult body (gross, disgusting)
Childlike emotions
Childlike voice
Choking/gagging
Claustrophobia
Compulsions
Constriction of normal bodily functions
Crying
Demon presence
Denial of sexual abuse
Depression
Downcast looks
Dreams of snakes
Dreams of spiders
Dying in a dream
Early childhood sexual drive
Early puberty
Emotional fear of Halloween
Emotional reaction to questions

Emotionally unstable spouse
Environmental disease
Excessive control by father in teens
Family secrets
Fear
Fear of being alone
Fear of black dogs
Fear of finding truth
Fear of knives
Fear of losing weight
Fear of rape
Fear of trusting God
Feeling dirty
Flashbacks, especially sexual
Fits of rage
Frozen emotions
Generational revisitation of abuse
Guilt
Habitual rectal itching
Hate homosexuals
Hate men
Hatred
Hiding face in hair
Hiding in a closet
Homosexuality
"I'm sorry" syndrome
Inability to call God "Father"
Inability to forgive
Inhibition to liquid medicine
Insecurity
Insomnia
Intense fear of child being abused
Interracial marriage
Jealousy
Known molestation
Lack of resistance to sexual attack
Late bedwetting
"Little mother" syndrome
Low self-worth
Lying/half-truths
Manic depressive
Marital sexual dysfunction
Marrying to escape
Masturbation
Memory gap
Mental flashes
Migraines
Missionary, social work
Molested others
Mood swings
Multiple clothing layers
Multiple divorces/marriages
Multiple personalities
Nail biting
Need light on to sleep
Negative thought patterns
Night terrors
No feelings
Obsessions
Obsessive-compulsive disorder
Out of touch with God
Overreactions
Overweight
Painful eyes
Panic attacks

Parent adoration
Parental preoccupation with sex
Phantoms in your life
Physical reaction to questions
PMS (PMD)
Poor opposite-sex relationships
Pornography at home
Post partum depression
Premature physical aging
Preoccupation with sex
Preoccupation with personal hygiene
Pulling out/cutting hair
Reaction to full moon
Reactive anger to hearing Scripture
Refusal to nurse baby
Rejection
Repugnance to oral sex
Repugnance to touching by opposite sex
Resentment
Self-deception
Self-destructive patterns
Self-hatred
Self-protection
Self-punishment
Sexual relieving of depression
Sleep disorder
Smells/odors reaction
"Something blocking me"
Split on personality profile
Strange feelings about "the cross"
Stress
Struggle for holiness
Suicidal feelings
Teenage promiscuity
Teenage runaway
Tension
Terrified of dentist
Threatened as child
TMJ
Traumatic reaction to abuse on film, TV
Trembling
Troubling memory fragments
Unbreakable strongholds
Uncontrollable crying as adult
Uncomfortable with nudity in marriage
Undiagnosed pains
Unexplained childhood vomiting
Unmet emotional needs
Unusual physical problems
Urge to molest
Use of drugs
Vaginal scars
Vaginismus
Workaholic

Appendix D

How to Know God Personally

Recently, at the Christian Booksellers Convention in Denver, Colorado, the cashier at one of the refreshment counters blurted out to me, "I'm jealous of all you Christians. You're all so happy."

"Aren't you a Christian?" I asked.

"No. God doesn't love me."

I was surprised by her frankness, but I realized that this attractive lady had deep hurts inside.

"When is your next break? I'd be happy to come back and talk with you."

"I have no idea," she replied. "I just came on duty."

I returned later to the refreshment counter, but someone else was working. I never saw the lonely lady again.

The message of this book is that Jesus came to save, to free and to heal people whose lives have been battered beyond hope.

> If you feel you are sinking and there is no hope,
>
> If you are not totally sure that one day you will stand in the presence of your heavenly Father,
>
> If you know you have hurts in your life, but you don't know how to communicate with the One who can help you, or
>
> If you have decided you want to know God personally,

then let this be the moment you make that life-transforming decision and tap into the life-changing power.

Jesus said, "For this is the will of My Father, that every one who beholds the Son, and believes in Him, may have eternal life; and I will raise him up on the last day" (John 6:40, NASB).

And John 1:12 promises: "As many as received Him, to them He gave the right to become children of God, even to those who believe in His name" (NASB).

Will you receive Him now? Will you receive from Him the free gift of eternal life that He is offering to you? Will you receive His power to repair your broken life?

If you answered yes, carefully and sincerely pray this simple prayer:

> "Dear Lord Jesus Christ, forgive me. I am a sinner. I have lived my life apart from You. I now wish to turn my life completely around and live it for You. I give myself to You. I receive You into my life. I believe that You are the risen Christ with the power to forgive my sins and transform my life. Today, begin Your work of healing in me. Thank You for hearing my prayer. Thank You for loving me just the way I am today. In the name of the Lord Jesus Christ, I commit myself to You. Amen."

If you prayed this prayer and truly meant it, you are now a member of the family of God. You are assured of your place in heaven. You have entered into a personal relationship with God and are ready to begin the lifelong journey of knowing Him intimately.

If you only *read* the prayer, go back now and *pray* the prayer. It is a choice you will never regret having made.

On this date, ____________________________, 19_____, I prayed and received Jesus Christ as Lord in my life.

Suggestions for Christian Growth

Spiritual growth results from trusting Jesus Christ. "The righteous man shall live by faith" (Galatians 3:11). A life of faith will enable you to trust God increasingly with every detail of your life, and to practice the following:

G Go to God in prayer daily (John 15:7).

R Read God's Word daily (Acts 17:11)—you may want to begin with the Gospel of John.

O Obey God moment by moment (John 14:21).

W Witness for Christ by your life and words (Matthew 4:19; John 15:8).

T Trust God for every detail of your life (1 Peter 5:7).

H Holy Spirit—Allow Him to control and empower your daily life and witness (Galatians 5:16,17; Acts 1:8).

God's Word also admonishes us not to forsake "the assembling of ourselves together" (Hebrews 10:25). Several logs burn brightly together, but put one aside on the cold hearth and the fire goes out. So it is with your relationship with other Christians. If you do not belong to a church, do not wait to be invited. Take the initiative; call the pastor of a nearby church where Christ is honored and His Word is preached. Start this week, and make plans to attend regularly.

Steven Pogue has written an excellent book designed to help you make the most of your new life in Christ. The title is *The First Year of Your Christian Life* (Here's Life Publishers) and it is available in Christian bookstores everywhere.

Appendix E

"I'M SPECIAL"

I'm special. In all the world there's nobody like me.

Since the beginning of time, there has never been another person like me. Nobody has my smile, nobody has my eyes, my nose, my hair, my hands, my voice . . . I'm special.

No one can be found who has my handwriting.

Nobody anywhere has my tastes for food or music or art . . . no one sees things just as I do.

In all of time there's been no one who laughs like me, no one who cries like me; and what makes me laugh and cry will never provoke identical laughter and tears from anybody else, ever.

No one reacts to any situation just as I would react. I'm special.

I'm the only one in all of creation who has my set of abilities. Oh, there will always be somebody who is better at one of the things I'm good at, but no one in the universe can reach the quality of my combination of talents, ideas, abilities and feelings. Like a room full of musical instruments, some may excel alone, but none can match the symphony sound when all are played together. I'm special.

Through all of eternity no one will ever look, talk, walk, think or do like me. I'm special. I'm rare.

And in all rarity there is great value.

Because of my rare value, I need not attempt to imitate others. I will accept—yes, celebrate—my differences.

I'm special and I'm beginning to realize it's no accident that I'm special. I'm beginning to see that *God* made me special for a very special purpose. He must have a job for me that no one else can do as well. Out of all the billions of applicants, only one is qualified, only one has the right combination of what it takes . . .

That one is me because . . . I'm special.

—Author Unknown

Appendix F

THE CRUCIFIXION OF JESUS: THE PASSION OF CHRIST FROM A MEDICAL POINT OF VIEW

Author Unknown

I shall discuss some of the physical aspects of the passion, or suffering, of Jesus Christ. We shall follow Him from Gethsemane, through His trial, His scourging, His path along the Via Dolorosa, to His last dying hours on the cross.

I became interested in this about a year ago when I read an account of the crucifixion in Jim Bishop's book, *The Day Christ Died.* I suddenly realized that I had taken the crucifixion more or less for granted all these years—that I had grown callous to its honor by a too easy familiarity with the grim details—and a too distant friendship with Him. It finally occurred to me that as a physician I didn't even know the actual immediate cause of death. The Gospel writers don't help us very much on this point because crucifixion and scourging were so common during their lifetime that they undoubtedly considered a detailed description totally superfluous—so we have the concise word of evangelists: "Pilate, having scourged Jesus, delivered Him to them to be crucified—and they crucified Him."

I am indebted to many who have studied this subject in the past, and especially to a contemporary colleague, Dr. Pieree Barbet, a French surgeon who has done exhaustive historical and experimental research and has written extensively on the subject.

The infinite psychic and spiritual suffering of the incarnate God in atonement for the sins of fallen men I have no competence to discuss. However, the physiological and anatomical aspects of our Lord's passion we can examine in some detail.

What did the body of Jesus of Nazareth actually endure during those hours of torture?

This led me first to a study of the practice of crucifixion itself: that is, the torture and execution of a person by fixation to a cross. Apparently, the first known practice of crucifixion was by the Persians. Alexander and his generals brought it back to the Mediterranean world—to Egypt and to Carthage. The Romans apparently learned the practice from the Carthaginians and (as with almost everything the Romans did) rapidly developed a very high degree of efficiency and skill in carrying it out. A number of Roman authors (Livy, Cicero, Tacitus) comment on it. Several innovations and modifications are described in the ancient literature; I'll mention only a few which may have some bearing here.

The upright portion of the cross (or stipes) could have the cross-arm (or patibulum) attached two or three feet below its top—this is what we commonly think as the classical form of the cross (the one which we have later named the Latin cross); however, the common form used in our Lord's day was the Tau cross (shaped like the Greek letter Tau or like our T). In this cross the patibulum was placed in a notch at the top of the stipes. There is fairly overwhelming archeological evidence that it was on this type of cross that Jesus was crucified.

The upright post, or stipes, was generally permanently fixed in the ground at the site of execution and the condemned man was forced to carry the patibulum, apparently weighing about 110 pounds, from the prison to the place of execution. Without any historical or biblical proof, medieval and Renaissance painters have given us our picture of Christ carrying the entire cross. Many of these painters and most of the sculptors of crucifixes today show the nails through the palms. Roman historical accounts and experimental work have shown that the nails were driven between the small bones of the wrists and not through the palms. Nails driven through the palms will strip out between the fingers when they support the weight of the human body. The misconception may have come through a misunderstanding of Jesus' words to Thomas, "Observe my hands."

Anatomists, both modern and ancient, have always considered the wrists as part of the hands.

A titulus, or small sign, stating the victim's crime was usually carried at the front of the procession and later nailed to the cross above the head. This sign with its staff nailed to the top of the cross would have given it somewhat the characteristic form of the Latin cross.

The physical passion of Christ begins in Gethsemane. Of the many aspects of this initial suffering, I shall only discuss the one of physiological interest—the bloody sweat. It is interesting that the physician of the group, St. Luke, is the only one to mention this. He says, "And being in agony, He prayed the longer. And His sweat became as drops of blood, trickling down upon the ground."

Every attempt imaginable has been used by modern scholars to explain away this phase, apparently under the mistaken impression that this just doesn't happen.

A great deal of effort could be saved by consulting the medical literature. Though very rare, the phenomenon of Hematidrosis, or bloody sweat, is well documented. Under great emotional stress, tiny capillaries in the sweat glands can break, thus mixing blood with sweat. This process alone could have produced marked weakness and possible shock.

We shall move rapidly through the betrayal and arrest. I must stress again that important portions of the Passion story are missing from this account. This may be frustrating to you, but in order to adhere to our purpose of discussing only the purely physical aspects of the Passion, this is necessary. After the arrest in the middle of the night, Jesus was brought before the Sanhedrin and Caiaphas, the High Priest. It is here that the first physical trauma was inflicted. A soldier struck Jesus across the face for remaining silent when questioned by Caiphas. The palace guards then blindfolded Him and mockingly taunted Him to identify them as they each passed by, spat on Him, and struck Him in the face.

In the early morning, Jesus, battered and bruised, dehydrated and exhausted from a sleepless night, is taken across Jerusalem to the Praetorium of the Fortress Antonia, the seat of government of the Procurator of Judea, Pontius Pilate. You are, of course, familiar with Pilate's action in attempting to pass responsibility to Herod Antipas, the Tetrarch of Judea. Jesus apparently suffered no physical mistreatment at the hands of Herod and was returned to Pilate. It was in response then to the cries of the mob, that Pilate ordered Bar-Abbas released and condemned Jesus to scourging and crucifixion. There is much disagreement among authorities about scourging as a prelude to crucifixion. Most Roman writers from this period do not associate the two. Many scholars believe that Pilate originally ordered Jesus scourged as His full punishment and that the death sentence of crucifixion came only in response to the taunt by the mob that the Procurator was not properly defending Caesar against this pretender who claimed to be the King of the Jews.

Preparations for the scourging were carried out. The prisoner is stripped of His clothing and His hands tied to a post above His head. It is doubtful whether the Romans made any attempt to follow the Jewish law in this matter of scourging. The Jews had an ancient law prohibiting more than forty lashes. The Pharisees, always making sure that the law was strictly kept, insisted that only thirty-nine lashes be given. (In case of a miscount, they were sure of remaining within the law.) The Roman legionnaire steps forward with the flagrum (or flagellum) in his hand. This is a short whip consisting of several heavy leather thongs with two small balls of lead attached near the ends of each. The heavy whip is brought down with full force across Jesus' shoulders, back and legs. At first the heavy thongs cut through the skin only.

Then, as the blows continue, they cut deeper into the subcutaneous tissues, producing first an oozing of blood from the capillaries and veins of skin, and finally spurting arterial bleeding from vessels in the underlying muscles. The small balls of lead first produce deep bruises which are broken open by subsequent blows. Finally the skin of the back is hanging in long ribbons and the entire area is an unrecognizable mass of torn, bleeding tissue. When it is determined by the centurion in charge that the prisoner is near death, the beating is finally stopped.

The half-fainting Jesus is then untied and allowed to slump to the stone pavement, wet with His own blood. The Roman soldiers see a great joke in this provincial Jew claiming to be a King. They throw a robe across His shoulders and place a stick in His hand for a scepter. They still need a crown to make their travesty complete. A bundle of flexible branches covered with long thorns (commonly used for firewood) are plaited into the shape of a crown and this is pressed into His scalp. Again there is copious bleeding (the scalp being one of the most vascular areas of the body). After mocking Him and striking Him across the face, the soldiers take the stick from His hand and strike Him across the head, driving thorns deeper into His scalp. Finally, they tire of their sadistic sport and the robe is torn from His back. This had already become adherent to the clots of blood and serum in the wounds, and its removal, just as in the careless removal of a surgical bandage, causes excruciating pain . . . almost as though He were again being whipped . . . and the wounds again began to bleed.

In deference to Jewish custom, the Romans return His garments. The heavy patibulum of the cross is tied across His shoulders, and the procession of the condemned Christ, two thieves and the execution detail of Roman soldiers headed by a centurion, begins its slow journey along the Via Dolorosa. In spite of His efforts to walk erect, the weight of the heavy wooden beam together with the shock produced by copious blood loss, is too much. He stumbles and falls. The rough wood of the beam gouges into the lacerated skin and muscles of the shoulders. He tries to rise, but human muscles have been pushed beyond their endurance. The Centurion, anxious to get on with the crucifixion, selects a stalwart North African onlooker, Simon of Cyrene, to carry the cross. Jesus follows, still bleeding and sweating the cold, clammy sweat of shock. The 650-yard journey from the fortress Antonia to Golgotha is finally completed. The prisoner is again stripped of His clothes—except for a loin cloth which is allowed the Jews.

The crucifixion begins. Jesus is offered wine mixed with Myrrh, a mild analgesic mixture. He refuses to drink. Simon is ordered to place the patibulum on the ground and Jesus is quickly thrown backward with His shoulders against the wood. The legionnaire feels for the depression at the front of the wrist.

He drives a heavy, square, wrought-iron nail through the wrist and deep into the wood. Quickly, he moves to the other side and repeats the action, being careful not to pull the arms too tightly, but to allow some flexion and movement. The patibulum is then lifted in place at the top of the stipes and the titulus reading "Jesus of Nazareth, the King of the Jews," is nailed in place.

The left foot is pressed backward against the right foot and with both feet extended, toes down, a nail is driven through the arch of each, leaving the knees moderately flexed. The victim is now crucified. As He slowly sags down with more weight on the nails in the wrists, excruciating, fiery pain shoots along the fingers and up the arms to explode in the brain—the nails in the wrists are putting pressure on the median nerves. As He pushes Himself upward to avoid this stretching torment, He places His full weight on the nail through His feet. Again there is the searing agony of the nail tearing through the nerves between the metatarsal bones of the feet.

At this point, another phenomenon occurs. As the arms fatigue, great waves of cramps sweep over the muscles, knotting them in deep, relentless, throbbing pain. With these cramps comes the inability to push Himself upward. Hanging by His arms, the pectoral muscles are paralyzed and the intercostal muscles are unable to act. Air can be drawn into the lungs, but cannot be exhaled. Jesus fights to raise Himself in order to get one short breath. Finally, carbon dioxide builds up in the lungs and in the blood stream and the cramps partially subside. Spasmodically, he is able to push Himself upward to exhale and bring in the life-giving oxygen.

It was undoubtedly during these periods that He uttered the seven short sentences which are recorded:

The first, looking down at the Roman soldiers throwing dice for His seamless garment, "Father, forgive them for they know not what they do."

The second, to the penitent thief, "Today thou shalt be with me in Paradise."

The third, looking down at the grief stricken, terrified adolescent John (the beloved apostle), He said, "Behold thy mother," and looking to Mary, His mother, "Woman, behold thy son."

The fourth cry is from the beginning of Psalm 22, "My God, my God, why hast thou forsaken me?"

Hours of this limitless pain, cycles of twisting, joint-rending cramps, intermittent partial asphyxiation, searing pain as tissue is torn from His lacerated back as He moves up and down against rough timber: Then another agony begins. A deep crushing pain in the chest as the pericardium slowly fills with serum and begins to compress the heart.

Let us remember again Psalm 22: "I am poured out like water, and all my bones are out of joint: my heart is like wax; it is melted in the midst of my bowels" (verse 14).

It is now almost over—the loss of tissue fluids has reached a critical level—the compressed heart is struggling to pump heavy, thick sluggish blood into the tissues—tortured lungs are making a frantic effort to gasp in small gulps of air. The markedly dehydrated tissues sent their flood of stimuli to the brain.

Jesus gasps His fifth cry, "I thirst."

Let us remember another verse from the prophetic Psalm 22: "My strength is dried up like a potsherd; and my tongue cleaveth to my jaws; and thou has brought me into the dust of death."

A sponge soaked in Posca, the cheap, sour wine which is the staple drink of the Roman legionnaires, is lifted to His lips. He apparently doesn't take any of the liquid. The body of Jesus is now in extremis, and He can feel the chill of death creeping through His tissue. This realization brings out His sixth words.

"It is finished."

His mission of atonement has been completed. Finally He can allow His body to die.

With one last surge of strength, He once again presses His torn feet against the nail, straightens His legs, takes a deeper breath, and utters His seventh and last cry.

"Father, into thy hands I commit my spirit."

The rest you know. In order that the Sabbath not be profaned, the Jews asked that the condemned men be dispatched and removed from the crosses. The common method of ending a crucifixion was by crucifracture, the breaking of the bones of the legs. This prevented the victim from pushing himself upward; the tension could not be relieved from the muscles of the chest, and rapid suffocation occurred. The legs of the two thieves were broken, but when the soldiers came to Jesus they saw that this was unnecessary.

Apparently to make doubly sure of death, one legionnaire drove his lance through the fifth interspace between the ribs, upward through the pericardium and into the heart. According to John 19:34: "And immediately there came out blood and water." Thus there was an escape of water fluid from the sac surrounding the heart and the blood from the interior of the heart. We, therefore, have rather conclusive post-mortem evidence that our Lord died, not the usual crucifixion death by suffocation, but of heart failure due to shock and constriction of the heart by fluid in the pericardium.

He did this for us. What have we done for Him? Amen.

Notes

Chapter 4: "I Never Felt Loved"

1. Stormie Omartian, *Virtue* (May/June 1989).
2. Barbara Taylor, *From Rejection to Acceptance* (Nashville, TN: Broadman Press, 1987), p. 48.
3. Taylor, p. 42.

Chapter 8: Other Significant Findings

1. See "Wounded Healers," *Atlantic Monthly* (February 1989).

Chapter 11: The Mirror of Your Soul

1. For a comprehensive and revealing look at the four basic personality types, see *Personality Plus* (Fleming H. Revell) and *Your Personality Tree* (Word Books), both by Florence Littauer.

Chapter 17: Benefits of Written Prayer

1. Oswald Chambers, *Christian Discipline, Vol. II* (Ft. Washington, PA: Christian Literature Crusade, 1936).
2. Oswald Chambers, *My Utmost for His Highest* (Westwood, NJ: Barbour & Co., Inc.), p. 329.
3. Chambers, *My Utmost for His Highest*, p. 118.

Chapter 20: "Forgive? How Can I?"

1. Patty McConnell, *A Workbook for Healing* (New York: Harper and Row, 1986).
2. Gerald G. Jampolsky, *Love Is Letting Go of Fear* (Millbrae, CA: n.pub., 1979).
3. Adapted from *How to Pray for Someone Near You Who Is Away From God* by Joy Dawson (Tujunga, CA).
4. Corrie Ten Boom, *The Hiding Place* (Old Tappan, NJ: Fleming Revell, 1971).